THE
CHINOOK

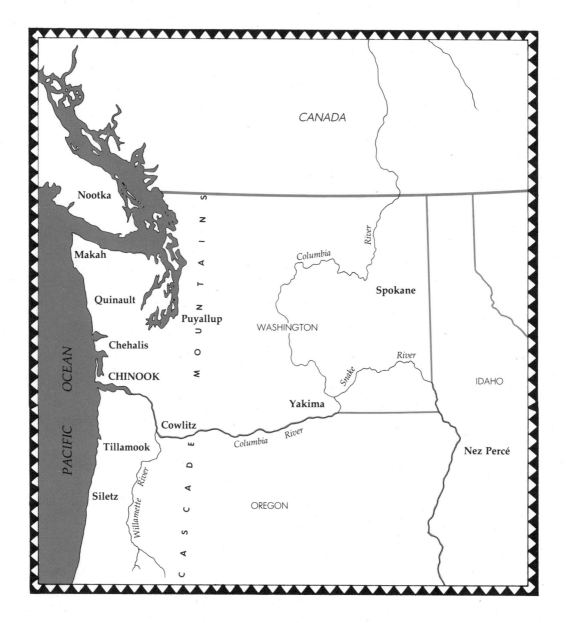

CANADA

PACIFIC OCEAN

Nootka

Makah

Quinault

Puyallup

Chehalis

CHINOOK

Cowlitz

Tillamook

Siletz

M O U N T A I N S

C A S C A D E

WASHINGTON

Columbia

River

Spokane

River

Snake

Yakima

Columbia River

OREGON

Willamette River

IDAHO

Nez Percé

THE
CHINOOK

Clifford E. Trafzer
San Diego State University

Frank W. Porter III
General Editor

CHELSEA HOUSE PUBLISHERS
New York   Philadelphia

On the cover An early-20th-century sheep-horn bowl with carved openwork handles.

Chelsea House Publishers
Editor-in-Chief Nancy Toff
Executive Editor Remmel T. Nunn
Managing Editor Karyn Gullen Browne
Copy Chief Juliann Barbato
Picture Editor Adrian G. Allen
Art Director Maria Epes
Manufacturing Manager Gerald Levine

Indians of North America
Senior Editor Liz Sonneborn

Staff for **THE CHINOOK**
Assistant Editor Claire M. Wilson
Deputy Copy Chief Nicole Bowen
Editorial Assistant Judith D. Weinstein
Assistant Art Director Loraine Machlin
Designer Donna Sinisgalli
Design Assistant James Baker
Picture Researcher Margalit Fox
Production Manager Joseph Romano
Production Coordinator Marie Claire Cebrián

First Printing

1 3 5 7 9 8 6 4 2

Library of Congress Cataloging-in-Publication Data

Trafzer, Clifford E.
  The Chinook / Clifford E. Trafzer.
    p. cm.—(Indians of North America)
  Includes bibliographical references.
  Summary: Examines the history, culture, changing fortunes, and current situation of the Chinook Indians.
  ISBN 1-55546-698-2
      0-7910-0373-6 (pbk.)
  1. Chinook Indians. [1. Chinook Indians. 2. Indians of North America.] I. Title. II. Series: Indians of North America (Chelsea House Publishers).
                                                89-36622
  E99.C57T73 1990   CIP
  973'.04974—dc20   AC

CONTENTS

INDIANS OF NORTH AMERICA

The Abenaki

American Indian
 Literature

The Apache

The Arapaho

The Archaeology
 of North America

The Aztecs

The Cahuilla

The Catawbas

The Cherokee

The Cheyenne

The Chickasaw

The Chinook

The Chipewyan

The Choctaw

The Chumash

The Coast Salish Peoples

The Comanche

The Creek

The Crow

The Eskimo

Federal Indian Policy

The Hidatsa

The Huron

The Iroquois

The Kiowa

The Kwakiutl

The Lenapes

The Lumbee

The Maya

The Menominee

The Modoc

The Montagnais-Naskapi

The Nanticoke

The Narragansett

The Navajo

The Nez Perce

The Ojibwa

The Osage

The Paiute

The Pima-Maricopa

The Potawatomi

The Powhatan Tribes

The Pueblo

The Quapaw

The Seminole

The Tarahumara

The Tunica-Biloxi

Urban Indians

The Wampanoag

Women in American
 Indian Society

The Yakima

The Yankton Sioux

The Yuma

CHELSEA HOUSE PUBLISHERS

INDIANS OF NORTH AMERICA: CONFLICT AND SURVIVAL

Frank W. Porter III

The Indians survived our open intention of wiping them out, and since the tide turned they have even weathered our good intentions toward them, which can be much more deadly.

John Steinbeck
America and Americans

When Europeans first reached the North American continent, they found hundreds of tribes occupying a vast and rich country. The newcomers quickly recognized the wealth of natural resources. They were not, however, so quick or willing to recognize the spiritual, cultural, and intellectual riches of the people they called Indians.

The Indians of North America examines the problems that develop when people with different cultures come together. For American Indians, the consequences of their interaction with non-Indian people have been both productive and tragic. The Europeans believed they had "discovered" a "New World," but their religious bigotry, cultural bias, and materialistic world view kept them from appreciating and understanding the people who lived in it. All too often they attempted to change the way of life of the indigenous people. The Spanish conquistadores wanted the Indians as a source of labor. The Christian missionaries, many of whom were English, viewed them as potential converts. French traders and trappers used the Indians as a means to obtain pelts. As Francis Parkman, the 19th-century historian, stated, "Spanish civilization crushed the Indian; English civilization scorned and neglected him; French civilization embraced and cherished him."

7

Nearly 500 years later, many people think of American Indians as curious vestiges of a distant past, waging a futile war to survive in a Space Age society. Even today, our understanding of the history and culture of American Indians is too often derived from unsympathetic, culturally biased, and inaccurate reports. The American Indian, described and portrayed in thousands of movies, television programs, books, articles, and government studies, has either been raised to the status of the "noble savage" or disparaged as the "wild Indian" who resisted the westward expansion of the American frontier.

Where in this popular view are the real Indians, the human beings and communities whose ancestors can be traced back to ice-age hunters? Where are the creative and indomitable people whose sophisticated technologies used the natural resources to ensure their survival, whose military skill might even have prevented European settlement of North America if not for devastating epidemics and disruption of the ecology? Where are the men and women who are today diligently struggling to assert their legal rights and express once again the value of their heritage?

The various Indian tribes of North America, like people everywhere, have a history that includes population expansion, adaptation to a range of regional environments, trade across wide networks, internal strife, and warfare. This was the reality. Europeans justified their conquests, however, by creating a mythical image of the New World and its native people. In this myth, the New World was a virgin land, waiting for the Europeans. The arrival of Christopher Columbus ended a timeless primitiveness for the original inhabitants.

Also part of this myth was the debate over the origins of the American Indians. Fantastic and diverse answers were proposed by the early explorers, missionairies, and settlers. Some thought that the Indians were descended from the Ten Lost Tribes of Israel, others that they were descended from inhabitants of the lost continent of Atlantis. One writer suggested that the Indians had reached North America in another Noah's ark.

A later myth, perpetrated by many historians, focused on the relentless persecution during the past five centuries until only a scattering of these "primitive" people remained to be herded onto reservations. This view fails to chronicle the overt and covert ways in which the Indians successfully coped with the intruders.

All of these myths presented one-sided interpretations that ignored the complexity of European and American events and policies. All left serious questions unanswered. What were the origins of the American Indians? Where did they come from? How and when did they get to the New World? What was their life—their culture—really like?

In the late 1800s, anthropologists and archaeologists in the Smithsonian Institution's newly created Bureau of American Ethnology in Washington,

D.C., began to study scientifically the history and culture of the Indians of North America. They were motivated by an honest belief that the Indians were on the verge of extinction and that along with them would vanish their languages, religious beliefs, technology, myths, and legends. These men and women went out to visit, study, and record data from as many Indian communities as possible before this information was forever lost.

By this time there was a new myth in the national consciousness. American Indians existed as figures in the American past. They had performed a historical mission. They had challenged white settlers who trekked across the continent. Once conquered, however, they were supposed to accept graciously the way of life of their conquerors.

The reality again was different. American Indians resisted both actively and passively. They refused to lose their unique identity, to be assimilated into white society. Many whites viewed the Indians not only as members of a conquered nation but also as "inferior" and "unequal." The rights of the Indians could be expanded, contracted, or modified as the conquerors saw fit. In every generation, white society asked itself what to do with the American Indians. Their answers have resulted in the twists and turns of federal Indian policy.

There were two general approaches. One way was to raise the Indians to a "higher level" by "civilizing" them. Zealous missionaries considered it their Christian duty to elevate the Indian through conversion and scanty education. The other approach was to ignore the Indians until they disappeared under pressure from the ever-expanding white society. The myth of the "vanishing Indian" gave stronger support to the latter option, helping to justify the taking of the Indians' land.

Prior to the end of the 18th century, there was no national policy on Indians simply because the American nation has not yet come into existence. American Indians similarly did not possess a political or social unity with which to confront the various Europeans. They were not homogeneous. Rather, they were loosely formed bands and tribes, speaking nearly 300 languages and thousands of dialects. The collective identity felt by Indians today is a result of their common experiences of defeat and/or mistreatment at the hands of whites.

During the colonial period, the British crown did not have a coordinated policy toward the Indians of North America. Specific tribes (most notably the Iroquois and the Cherokee) became military and political pawns used by both the crown and the individual colonies. The success of the American Revolution brought no immediate change. When the United States acquired new territory from France and Mexico in the early 19th century, the federal government wanted to open this land to settlement by homesteaders. But the Indian tribes that lived on this land had signed treaties with European governments assuring their title to the land. Now the United States assumed legal responsibility for honoring these treaties.

At first, President Thomas Jefferson believed that the Louisiana Purchase contained sufficient land for both the Indians and the white population. Within a generation, though, it became clear that the Indians would not be allowed to remain. In the 1830s the federal government began to coerce the eastern tribes to sign treaties agreeing to relinquish their ancestral land and move west of the Mississippi River. Whenever these negotiations failed, President Andrew Jackson used the military to remove the Indians. The southeastern tribes, promised food and transportation during their removal to the West, were instead forced to walk the "Trail of Tears." More than 4,000 men, woman, and children died during this forced march. The "removal policy" was successful in opening the land to homesteaders, but it created enormous hardships for the Indians.

By 1871 most of the tribes in the United States had signed treaties ceding most or all of their ancestral land in exchange for reservations and welfare. The treaty terms were intended to bind both parties for all time. But in the General Allotment Act of 1887, the federal government changed its policy again. Now the goal was to make tribal members into individual landowners and farmers, encouraging their absorption into white society. This policy was advantageous to whites who were eager to acquire Indian land, but it proved disastrous for the Indians. One hundred thirty-eight million acres of reservation land were subdivided into tracts of 160, 80, or as little as 40 acres, and allotted tribe members on an individual basis. Land owned in this way was said to have "trust status" and could not be sold. But the surplus land—all Indian land not allotted to individuals—was opened (for sale) to white settlers. Ultimately, more than 90 million acres of land were taken from the Indians by legal and illegal means.

The resulting loss of land was a catastrophe for the Indians. It was necessary to make it illegal for Indians to sell their land to non-Indians. The Indian Reorganization Act of 1934 officially ended the allotment period. Tribes that voted to accept the provisions of this act were reorganized, and an effort was made to purchase land within preexisting reservations to restore an adequate land base.

Ten years later, in 1944, federal Indian policy again shifted. Now the federal government wanted to get out of the "Indian business." In 1953 an act of Congress named specific tribes whose trust status was to be ended "at the earliest possible time." This new law enabled the United States to end unilaterally, whether the Indians wished it or not, the special status that protected the land in Indian tribal reservations. In the 1950s federal Indian policy was to transfer federal responsibility and jurisdiction to state governments, encourage the physical relocation of Indian peoples from reservations to urban areas, and hasten the termination, or extinction, of tribes.

Between 1954 and 1962 Congress passed specific laws authorizing the termination of more than 100 tribal groups. The stated purpose of the termination policy was to ensure the full and complete integration of Indians into American society. However, there is a less benign way to interpret this legislation. Even as termination was being discussed in Congress, 133 separate bills were introduced to permit the transfer of trust land ownership from Indians to non-Indians.

With the Johnson administration in the 1960s the federal government began to reject termination. In the 1970s yet another Indian policy emerged. Known as "self-determination," it favored keeping the protective role of the federal government while increasing tribal participation in, and control of, important areas of local government. In 1983 President Reagan, in a policy statement on Indian affairs, restated the unique "government is government" relationship of the United States with the Indians. However, federal programs since then have moved toward transferring Indian affairs to individual states, which have long desired to gain control of Indian land and resources.

As long as American Indians retain power, land, and resources that are coveted by the states and the federal government, there will continue to be a "clash of cultures," and the issues will be contested in the courts, Congress, the White House, and even in the international human rights community. To give all Americans a greater comprehension of the issues and conflicts involving American Indians today is a major goal of this series. These issues are not easily understood, nor can these conflicts be readily resolved. The study of North American Indian history and culture is a necessary and important step toward that comprehension. All Americans must learn the history of the relations between the Indians and the federal government, recognize the unique legal status of the Indians, and understand the heritage and cultures of the Indians of North America.

The interior of a Chinook lodge in an 1841 engraving by American artist A. T. Agate. Such large dwellings often housed several families.

1

TRADERS
OF THE
COLUMBIA

Northwestern Oregon and southeastern Washington grow very cold in the winter. During those months, the Chinook, who inhabited the region for hundreds of years, traditionally spent a great deal of time indoors. Their homes, which could hold several families, were long and rectangular and made of cedar planks and posts. Inside each dwelling was a large room heated by a fire in the center of the floor. On nights when the winds howled and the rains poured, everyone gathered there to hear one of the elders tell a story. Usually, the story described the ancient days of the Chinook. All those present listened carefully.

Children paid especially close attention because now and then an elder would ask one of them to repeat a particular story. The boy or girl who was chosen had to retell the story exactly as he or she had heard it; mistakes were not allowed. This system of exact repetition enabled the Chinook to make sure that their lore, which did not exist in written form, was passed on accurately.

The stories that made up the Chinook's oral tradition dealt with many topics. None was more important than the legend of how the Chinook people came to be. This story has been handed down from generation to generation. The Chinook today still remember it and tell it to their children.

According to the story, Old Man South Wind long ago was traveling north along the coast of the Pacific Ocean and eventually neared the mouth of the Columbia River. There he met Giant Woman and told her he was hungry. Giant Woman had no food, but she lent him an enormous net and explained he could catch fish in it. Old Man South Wind took the net and headed for the gray waters of the Pacific.

When he got there, he unfolded the net and dragged it along the ocean floor until he caught a fish. It was not an ordinary fish but a small whale, which Old Man South Wind brought ashore and began to cut. Giant Woman, who was present at the scene, instructed him to slice the whale lengthwise, from head to tail. But Old Man South Wind was so famished that he ignored Giant Woman and, because it was quicker, drew the knife over the arc of the whale's back, from side to side. Suddenly, the whale turned into a monstrous bird.

The bird then rose into the air, flapping wings so powerful that they shook the earth. As he climbed, Bird Monster blotted out the sun. Soon Old Man South Wind and Giant Woman saw that it was really Thunderbird. They were in awe of this great bird as they watched it fly to the mouth of the Columbia.

There, atop Saddle Mountain, Thunderbird built a large nest and laid several eggs in it. One day when Thunderbird flew away, Giant Woman climbed high to the bird's nest. She mischievously cracked an egg, but it was bad, and she threw it down the mountain. She cracked another and another until she had broken them all and hurled them from the peak. Each time an egg landed at the base of the moun-

tain, it became an Indian. This was how the first Chinook men, women, and children came to be.

The geographical features included in this legend hold keys to the history of the Chinook people. For example, the Columbia River, where Old Man South Wind meets Giant Woman, was for centuries the exclusive domain of the Chinook. Indeed, the word *Chinook*, which originated in the language of the Chehalis Indians, referred to a village located at the mouth of the Chinook River at Bakers Bay in what is now Washington State.

The name Chinook spread among other Indian peoples and gradually became the term for the four distinct groups who lived at the mouth of the Columbia River. These groups were the Clatsop, Kathlamet, Shoalwater Chinook, and Columbia Chinook. The members of each group viewed themselves as an independent people even though they were collectively called the Chinook. All spoke different dialects of the same language, but they shared a similar culture.

The Chinook were very religious. Like most other peoples, they believed in an unseen spiritual force that helped people throughout their life. Children learned from their parents, grandparents, and other relatives that the presence of this force could be felt in all things.

Chinook individuals discovered their own spirit power through a ritual known as a vision quest. When Chinook boys or girls reached the age of

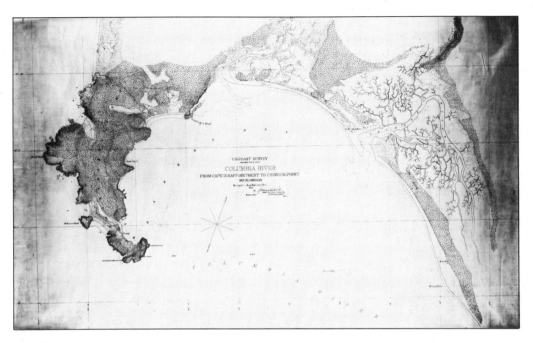

An 1869 U.S. Coast Survey map of the mouth of the Columbia River. The Columbia runs right through the heart of the Chinook's traditional homeland.

10, their elders gave the child a stick and instructed him or her to take it and travel alone to a certain sacred place some distance away, usually near a body of water. When the child arrived there, he or she placed the stick in the ground to mark the sacred spot and waited for a vision to appear. According to the elders' instructions, the person on the quest passed the time by swimming, diving, and shouting. The child continued to do this without food for as long as five days.

When the vision came, it often took the form of an animal, bird, whirlwind, or cloud. The spirit did not have a fixed form. At first it might resemble a mountain lion and then swiftly turn into a man. Soon after it appeared, the spirit spoke and explained that the young person had particular characteristics that would determine his or her role as an adult. It might tell a boy that he had the characteristics of a mountain lion and that he was destined to become a great hunter. A girl might learn that she would develop into a successful trader. The guardian spirit might also teach the child a special song or dance that could be used to summon the person's special power.

In rare instances, the guardian spirit informed a child that he or she was destined to become a healer, an important position in Chinook culture. The young person so instructed served an apprenticeship with a medicine man or woman for approximately five years. At the end of this period, the apprentice was ready to practice alone. A novice healer had to master the use of certain songs, prayers, and messages to diagnose and cure the ailing. Medicine men and women also were expected to be able to find missing people and to contact a dead person's spirit. Sometimes they were hired to cause harm to a patient's enemy through witchcraft. Most healers preferred to heal the sick, but their power to cause good or evil led the Chinook to fear as well as revere them.

One of the best-remembered Chinook stories concerns a male witch who was known for his "knife power,"

Interior of a Ceremonial Lodge, Columbia River, *painted in 1846 by Paul Kane, a Canadian artist who traveled throughout the Pacific Northwest in the mid-1840s. The Chinook Secret Society performed rituals in lodges such as this one.*

which allowed him to wound people through the craft of medicine. He wielded his power often and against whomever he liked. But once he picked the wrong target, a medicine woman. She, who had great powers of her own, suspected the witch was plotting to cut her with his knife power. In order to thwart him, she summoned her own special power, "hunting power," symbolized by her bow and arrow.

Both healers belonged to the Chinook Secret Society, and during a ceremony held by the society, the two agreed to a contest to see which medicine person was the more powerful. The medicine woman was sent alone into a room of a large ceremonial house, while the man stayed with the rest of the members. They looked on as he hid his magic knife from view. Then several members left to fetch the woman. When she joined the group, she was instructed to find the hidden knife. First she performed a ceremonial dance, brandishing her bow and arrow. She quickly found the knife, stuck it in the wall, and danced while shooting arrows at it. She hit the knife every time.

She then left the room, and again the witch hid his knife, this time in the sand by the fire that burned in the center of the large room. Once again the medicine woman was led into the room—this time blindfolded. She danced, drew her bow, and sent an arrow into the sand exactly where the knife was hidden.

The woman left the room a third time, and once again the witch hid his knife. The medicine woman returned, promptly lay on her back, and aimed her bow at the ceiling. An arrow clanged against the hidden knife. Thoroughly shamed, the witch fled the ceremonial lodge and dropped his plans for using his knife power against his gifted rival.

Medicine people were not the only Chinook to make public displays of their spirit power. On many occasions, the Chinook gathered together to celebrate the unseen forces that guided their lives. One such event was the Spirit Dance, which was held annually sometime between September and March as part of the Guardian Spirit Ceremony. It usually lasted five days— a sacred number to the Chinook. During that time, people who had discovered their spirit power sang and danced in the manner prescribed by their guardian spirit when they had first seen it.

The Guardian Spirit Ceremony also gave ill people the chance to try special cures developed by healers. The cures, administered during a ceremony, sometimes involved the use of two "power sticks"—each 10 feet long— and flat, diamond-shaped cedar planks known as "power boards." Healers called on spirits through dance, song, and prayer and asked them to improve the condition of various patients. Legend holds that during one such ceremony a man who had been blind for three years regained his sight.

Medicine people, because of their remarkable powers, often held high

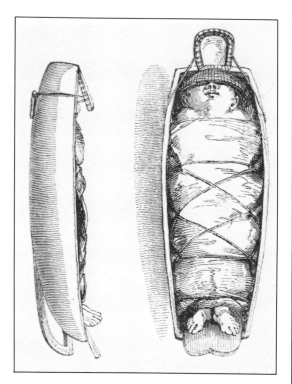

An 1839 engraving of a Chinook infant secured in a cradleboard. Pressure applied by the wooden plate above its head flattened the front of the child's skull. A flattened forehead was a sign of beauty in traditional Chinook society.

rank within Chinook society, but not always. Like many peoples, the Chinook greatly emphasized lineage; few individuals rose above their parents' social station. There were four major Chinook classes and little movement between them: upper class, commoners, lower class, and slaves. There were exceptions, however. If a man or woman became a great healer, for example, he or she might gain entry into the upper class. And once, a talented

gambler who had won the property of many chiefs and other members of the upper class was permitted to join their ranks. They believed that he had an especially powerful guardian spirit and thus deserved an honored place within the tribe.

All chiefs belonged to the upper class. The son of one chief usually became a chief himself and ruled over the population of an entire village. A few chiefs extended their influence into neighboring villages, but they held the greatest power over people near their home. When a fisherman brought his catch or a hunter brought game back to a village, the chief had the right to divide it among his people as he saw fit. If a chief chose, he could take for himself all the animals or fish caught by another man and leave the hunter or fisherman with nothing. Chiefs also had the power to sell orphaned children into slavery.

Slavery was practiced by many of the Indians who lived on the Northwest coast. The Chinook kept numerous slaves. Some they purchased from other tribes; others they seized in raids on Indian enemies. The members of the three free Chinook classes could all own slaves, but most slave owners belonged to the upper class. The typical member of the upper class usually owned between two and four slaves.

Slaves did much of the Chinook's work, including fishing, hunting, cooking, canoeing, gathering wild plants, and woodcutting. Slaves were also used as a means of exchange and investment and were given as gifts. Sometimes slaves who were bought or captured from other tribes could win their freedom by gaining wealth or by performing an unusual and important service for their master, such as saving the master's life. But those born into slavery could not improve their position. Often slaves were killed when their owners died.

Visitors who came to know the Chinook could immediately spot the slaves among them because they were the only villagers who had not been treated to an important Chinook method of beautification—head flattening. For at least a year, all free Chinook infants were placed in a special cradleboard that applied pressure to the front of the babies' soft skull. When children were taken out of this device, their foreheads were permanently sloped. Head flattening evidently did not impair a child's mental abilities, for the Chinook were widely admired for their keen intellects.

Life in Chinook villages was stable and secure. Parents poured attention on their children, and grandparents and other relatives helped rear them. Boys and girls imitated their parents in work and play. Both spent a good deal of time swimming, diving, and canoeing. When they were old enough, girls helped their mothers gather food, water, and wood, and boys helped their fathers fish, hunt, and build homes. Although slaves performed many of these jobs, families taught their children the value of hard work. Even upper-class adults and children often fished,

hunted game, and gathered wild plants alongside their slaves.

The Chinook were great fishermen and enjoyed the bounty of the Pacific Ocean. The portion of their catch that they did not eat themselves they traded to other Indians, who relished the salmon, sturgeon, steelhead, smelt, sardines, candlefish, herring, and other fish the Chinook caught. Their tools for catching fish included large sieve nets, dip nets, and spears. They also used weirs—wooden fences that were used to dam narrow rivers and streams and trap fish so that they could be grabbed or easily netted. Chinook fishermen nabbed giant sturgeon with wooden fishhooks and then, bare-handed, fought and landed the 15-foot, 300- or 400-pound fish. The Chinook revered the salmon and sturgeon. Each year they held thanksgiving ceremonies in honor of these fish and the Creator who provided them.

The Chinook also gathered huge quantities of oysters, clams, and cockles. The Indians dug clams out of the wet, sandy beaches with their hands or with wooden digging sticks with cupped shovels at one end. They cooked the clams they collected in a special way. First they placed rocks in a roaring fire until they grew hot. Then they removed the red-hot rocks and placed the clams on top of them. The heat caused the clams to open, and out spilled juices that turned into steam. The Chinook then placed mats over the clams to trap the steam, and the clams cooked as if inside an oven. The Chinook even found a use for the leftover shells. Once the meat was removed, they cured and dried the shells and sold them to other Indians.

The sea also provided the Chinook with a wealth of mammals. The Chinook hunted seals, sea lions, sea otters, and—most common of all—hair seals. These creatures sunbathed on the beaches near Chinook villages and sometimes grew up to 100 pounds. Chinook men usually hunted them with a spear that measured 20 feet long. Each spear was made of a wooden shaft and a detachable stone head attached to a long line of sinew. When the hunter plunged the spear into the seal's body, the head separated from the shaft. A spear shaft, therefore, could be used again and again.

Hunters approached the seals by canoe, landing downwind from the animals as they lounged on the beach. Each hunter wound the sinew line around his body, gripped the excess line in his left hand, and held the long spear in his right. He then slipped into the shallow water and floated facedown, his head bobbing just below the water's surface. As he moved toward his catch, he lifted his head so that his long hair floated around his face. From a distance, he resembled a seal. When he was close enough to strike his prey, he suddenly rose above the seal with his spear held high. He leapt to his feet and brought the spear down into the animal's flesh. The hunter then braced his body and held the sinew tightly to prevent the dying seal from escaping out to sea.

The Chinook also savored whale meat. According to Chinook lore, their ancestors steered canoes far into the Pacific in search of gray whales, sperm whales, and pollack whales. In most cases, however, the whales they found had washed ashore. Either way, the Chinook made excellent use of every part of the animal. They butchered the whales for their meat, blubber, and oil. A single whale could feed many mouths for several months.

Chinook hunters were skilled on land as well as on sea. They lived in a forested region thick with animals. Elk, deer, and bear offered the best meat, but the Chinook also tracked down raccoons, squirrels, minks, rabbits, bobcats, mountain lions, and porcupines. Hunters used sinew-backed bows, arrows, nets, and clubs to pursue ducks, snipes, and beavers. The Indians ate all of these animals but refused to eat eels, turtles, and frogs. They also probably did not eat wolf, owl, eagle, crow, sea gull, and raven.

The plant life in Chinook country was equally rich. The nutritious roots of the lupine, bracken fern, edible thistle, and horsetail rush grew wild in the area. The forests teemed with many edible berries, including salmonberries, strawberries, blueberries, huckleberries, blackberries, cranberries, and many others. There were also grapes, currants, crab apples, cow parsnips, and wild celery.

The Chinook either gathered these foods or traded for them. Women, who did most of the cooking, varied their meals to provide a balanced diet for their families. They also smoked fish and sun-dried meat, vegetables, and fruit so that these preserved foods could be eaten year-round. The resources of the region where the Chinook lived were so plenteous that they did not have to farm. The animals and plants in their environment gave them an ample food supply.

The Chinook did not gather, hunt, and fish only to obtain food. They also performed these activities in order to get materials that they could sew into mats, baskets, and clothing. The Chinook tanned the skins of sea otter, beaver, elk, deer, and bear by scraping, stretching, and smoking them to produce beautiful hides. These hides were ideal for blankets, bedding, and clothing. They used small rushes to make water-repellent robes and cedar bark to make skirts. Chinook women also wove basket hats from dyed strips of cedar bark, spruce root, and bear grass. These waterproof hats were worn by both men and women, and the colorful and intricate woven designs on the hats made them favored trade items.

The Chinook traded to other tribes any excess food or handmade objects

Catching Salmon on the Columbia River, *painted in 1846 by Paul Kane. Fishing, collecting shellfish, and hunting sea mammals provided the Chinook with much of their food and many of their trade goods.*

A bag made from rushes by a Clatsop Indian. The Clatsop and the Chinook were skilled weavers, and their woven goods were highly prized as trade items.

they produced. Commerce dominated Chinook life. Men and women both were involved in it; women often made names for themselves and their families as outstanding traders. Aside from trade's economic benefits, it brought the Chinook in contact with many other Indian groups and therefore formed the basis of social, business, and military alliances with other peoples.

Originally the Chinook's principal trade item was dentalia shells that were used as currency on the Northwest coast and portions of the Columbia Plateau. These shells could not be found south of the Strait of Juan de Fuca (which connects what is now Washington State with British Columbia, Canada), but the Chinook, who could trade for the shells with northern Indians, controlled the market in them. They also dealt heavily in the slave trade and nearly cornered the market on food items that they dried and smoked, including shellfish, salmon, sturgeon, smelt, and seal. The Chinook specialized in two other important items—blubber and canoes.

This last commodity was essential. Trade would not have been possible without a reliable means of transportation. The Chinook built canoes or obtained them through trade with the Nootka Indians of Vancouver Island. The Nootka often had carved animals and human figures on the prows of their vessels. The largest canoe the Chinook used measured a full 50 feet in length. It could carry as many as 30 people and cargo weighing as much as 10,000 pounds.

Special craftsmen among the Chinook made canoes from white cedar or fir trees. The builder first dug out the core of the tree, filled it with water, and then placed hot rocks inside. This made the wood pliable. Using wooden rods, the craftsman spread the interior of the boat outward so that the top edge of the canoe flared out, forming a lip that would keep water from entering the vessel. These canoes were meant to be used not only in rivers but also in bays and even in the choppy, open waters of the Pacific.

For most local travel, especially on their frequent trips from the Columbia River to Shoalwater Bay, the Chinook skirted the ocean and instead followed the south fork of the Naselle River. They paddled into the ocean, however, when they trekked north and south and up the Columbia River. Sometimes the Chinook used the canoes to conduct warfare, but they were primarily trade vehicles.

In order to expand their markets and control many trade items, the Chinook developed a unique trade dialect known as the Chinook Jargon. Many tribes on the Northwest coast used this language, and the Chinook enriched it through their trade dealings. After Europeans began to arrive in their territory in the 18th century, the Chinook added Spanish, English, and Russian words to the jargon. The language grew as new trade items or terms were introduced to the Indians. Eventually, the Chinook provided the common language of the Northwest trade, one used by Indians and non-Indians alike.

Long before the arrival of the first white men, the Chinook had established a successful way of life. Chinook men and women were accomplished traders, and their canoes kept the com-

A Chinook canoe photographed in 1910 by Edward S. Curtis. The Chinook's success as traders was wholly dependent on canoes, which they used to travel to neighboring villages and trading posts.

merce moving among their Indian neighbors. The visits of the first non-Indian traders to the region would signal a new era for the Chinook, one in which their reputation as business people would grow even greater. ▲

A 1791 painting of the Columbia (left), after which the Columbia River was named. Robert Gray, the captain of the American ship, did little to foster good-will among the Indians of the Pacific Northwest—he burned villages and fired on their inhabitants.

THE ARRIVAL
OF THE
SUYAPEE

Chinook oral tradition records the Indians' first meeting with whites. The story begins when a Chinook woman mourning the death of her son left her home for the first time in a year to take a walk among the tall green trees of the forest. During her lonely excursion, she went to the beach. As she gazed out at the Pacific Ocean, she saw a strange object bobbing up and down in the waves.

From a distance it resembled a whale. But as it drew nearer, its shape changed. When it landed on the beach, it appeared to be a monster with two giant spruces planted in its body and strung with many ropes that had evidently sprouted from the monster's back. Also on the back of the monster stood two hairy animals, probably bears, although their faces seemed to be human.

The woman was terrified by this sight but also astonished. She stared at it for a while and then ran back to her village to tell her people. The villagers grew excited when the woman described the monster and the bearlike animals with thick black hair on their face. She told the men in the village exactly where the monster had landed and offered to lead them there. The warriors then armed themselves with bows and arrows to be prepared in the event that the monster and bears were unfriendly.

True to her word, the woman led the warriors to the "creatures" she had seen—a large ship with two white men aboard. When they saw the Indians, they held up copper kettles and made

A Kathlamet woman photographed in the early 1900s. She is wearing a cape decorated with rows of dentalia shells—highly sought-after trade items in Chinook society.

signs with their hands to indicate that they wanted water. One brave Chinook boarded the ship and was greeted by the whites in a friendly manner. The Indian saw that the deck of the ship held many wooden boxes and several brass buttons—objects completely new to him. In his excitement, he signaled for the other warriors to join him on board. But in a panic they had already set fire to the huge craft. The warrior and two white men left the boat and went ashore.

Word of the ship and the two white men spread through the region. Many people wanted a look at the "monster" and "bears." The Indians were fasci-

nated by one of the bearded white men, who was bald; he looked particularly strange to the Chinook because their men had little facial growth and rarely lost their hair. They called the man *Suyapee*—or "upside-down face." Today, many Indians of the Northwest refer to white people as Suyapee or Suyapo.

After the flames died on the white men's ship, the Chinook took its cargo and traded many items to other Indian tribes. Metals, such as copper, iron, and brass, were soon in great demand. A single nail could be traded for a tanned deerskin. A small piece of brass bought an expensive slave. A few nails fetched a long string of precious dentalia. Trading would never be the same in North America.

No one knows exactly when this ship and the others that soon followed landed on the Pacific coast. It is likely, however, that the sailors came from China or Japan, their long trip made possible by the guiding winds and currents of the Pacific. Archaeologists have found Asian artifacts on the coast, which suggest that Asians traded with Northwestern Indians, but the extent and nature of the trade remains a mystery.

Later—in the 18th and 19th centuries—British and American traders reached the Pacific Northwest by traveling overland from the colonies and posts they had established on the east coast of North America. But before then, the Chinook continued the busy trade relations they had established with Indians to the north, such as the

Nootka, Haida, and Kwakiutl. Dentalia, canoes, and wooden tools formed the basis of exchange. The Chinook also traded with the Indians of present-day California for tobacco and Oregon for slaves. Some Chinook traders traveled inland to the Columbia Plateau, Rocky Mountains, and Great Plains. Often they traded finely pounded dry salmon, packed in 90-pound baskets made of rushes and salmon skin, for buffalo meat, hides, and long-stem pipes.

Indeed, the Chinook traveled so much and so far that they probably dealt with European traders before John Meares, the first European known to land in the area, dropped anchor in Shoalwater Bay in July 1788. The British sea captain arrived in a vessel packed with trade items. Meares soon returned to England, but he told few people there about his trade with the Chinook. He had not been granted a license from the English government to trade on the Northwest coast and so kept his business secret. However, he did record in his journal that the Chinook excelled at trading, an opinion echoed later by other ship captains who dealt with them.

One reason Meares had come to Chinook country was to trade with the Indians for sea-otter pelts. Earlier voyagers to the Northwest coast, from Spain and England, had obtained these furs and taken them to China, where they could be sold for fabulous prices. The Chinese prized fine sea-otter pelts and sewed them into fur capes, coats, mittens, sashes, and belts. News of how much the Chinese valued these furs spread after the voyages of British navy captain James Cook, who had traded for the pelts on his third expedition to the Northwest in the late 1770s. When he arrived in China, he exchanged his cargo for the equivalent of $120 a fur—an astounding price. He reported this success, and others sought to duplicate his feat. In the next several years, English captains James Hanna and Charles Barkley guided ships to the Northwest and traded for sea-otter furs with Indians living north of the Chinook. They did not match the profits made by Cook, but they did well

In the mid-1700s, British navy captain James Cook led several successful trading expeditions to the Pacific Northwest. His acquisition of valuable Indian goods inspired other non-Indian traders to come to the region.

enough to inspire other traders, including Meares.

Sea otters are sleek, webbed-footed animals that glide swiftly in the waters of the Northwest. As adults, they measure five feet in length and have fur that falls loosely around their bodies. When the Indians learned that the European traders wanted these creatures, they began killing large numbers of them and swapping them with whites for a small number of goods. Once the Indians learned how much foreign traders valued the furs, however, they drove a much harder bargain.

Meares became the first European known to have traded with the Chinook, but he fell short of his true goal—finding the great river that would allow him to travel easily by water into the interior of the continent, to trade with the Indians there. Other sea captains had reported that such a river existed, but no one had found it. Meares doggedly sought the river, and when he failed to locate it, he gave the name Cape Disappointment to a rocky point near where he had expected the river to be. He sailed away, unaware that he had in fact found the entrance to the Columbia River—the very waterway for which he had been searching.

A few years later, in 1792, an American, Captain Robert Gray, entered the mouth of the river. The captain commanded the 212-ton ship *Columbia*, which he had loaded with trade goods before sailing to the Northwest coast. Gray first landed in Adventure Cove on Vancouver Island. There he fought with the Indians he met and set their village afire. His men burned 200 homes, many containing priceless wooden carvings.

Word of Gray's crime spread among the Indians of the Northwest as he traveled south to the Washington coast. He did not improve his reputation when he fired rifles at Indians at a point later named Grays Harbor.

Gray was well known to the Chinook by May 11, 1792, the date he crossed the dangerous sand bar at the mouth of the Columbia River and sailed into the wide, treacherous waterway. The Chinook gathered on the riverbank to watch the huge ship nosing inland. Some Chinook climbed into their canoes and trailed his vessel, being as quiet as possible, because they feared Gray might harm them. After about 10 miles, the *Columbia* dropped anchor outside a large Indian village. Later, whites named this town Chinook Village. Some of the Indians there had never seen such a large ship and thought, like the grieving mother in the legend, that it was an overgrown monster. Many Chinook, including a chief named Polack, ventured out to greet the sailors.

Gray, it turned out, was on a peaceful trading mission. He swapped nails, spikes, cloth, copper, thimbles, and buttons for sea- and land-otter pelts, which the Chinook had in good supply. They also traded beaver furs, salmon, and roots. The exchange went well; both parties were pleased. The close contact provided the Americans with an opportunity to observe the Chinook briefly and to write about their culture. One member of the expedition, John Boit, recorded his observations of the Chinook and provided some insights into Chinook life in his log.

Boit noted that numerous Chinook Indians lived along the Columbia River. He judged them to be "civil" and generally friendly to whites and, as a people, to be generous and industrious. Boit wrote that most Chinook were heavyset and short, the men averaging about five and a half feet tall. They had relatively light skin and broad faces.

Some Chinook pierced their ears and wore jewelry made of dentalia, copper, and beads. Boit particularly marveled at their practice of head flattening.

Boit also admired the Chinook's solidly constructed homes. He noted that they were made of durable cedar posts and beams, and he described the Chinook's building methods. The Indians split cedar trunks into planks that were usually two inches thick and two feet wide. These planks formed the walls and roofs of their rectagular homes. They always made gabled, or steeply

A painting of Cape Disappointment, which was named by British captain John Meares. He had hoped to find the entrance to the Columbia River at the cape but was unable to do so.

sloped, roofs that funneled away rain-water. The Chinook entered their homes through oval doorways located just above ground level at one or both of the two smaller sides of the dwelling.

The Indians kept cold winds and rain from entering the houses by hanging door planks above these entrances. Someone coming inside the house pushed aside the plank, which then swung back into place. Village artists painted door planks and the surrounding walls. They typically covered these walls with an image of a human or animal figure whose mouth was formed by the door opening. The door plank was then painted to match. Inside the Chinook's homes were platforms for sitting, sleeping, and storage.

Boit wrote that when women were outdoors they carried their infants in cradleboards. While indoors, they often used ropes to suspend the cradleboards from the rafters. As the cradleboards turned around slowly on the ropes, babies could watch their mothers prepare roots, berries, and salmon for supper and their fathers haul in firewood. Dangling high above the activity of the home, babies were soothed and amused. With infants so occupied, parents were free to do their own work.

The Chinook had a term for American sailors such as John Boit and Captain Gray: "Boston Men." The term referred to the men on the great number of trading ships that sailed from Boston Harbor off the coast of Massachusetts. The Chinook also had their own name for British traders, "King George Men," a reference to King George III, the English monarch during the late 18th and early 19th centuries.

The first King George Men to enter the Columbia River arrived only a few months after Gray. In October 1792,

A 20th-century mural in the state capitol in Salem, Oregon, depicting the arrival of American sea captain Robert Gray at Chinook Village.

An 1841 engraving, by A. T. Agate, of two Chinook women seated beside an infant in a traditional cradleboard.

Captain James Baker navigated his 78-ton schooner *Jenny* up the bar. He had sailed a short distance upriver when three canoes with Chinook traders paddled out to meet him. They offered salmon, but seemed uninterested in trading anything else, probably because they had no other surplus goods. Baker anchored his ship in a bay near the mouth of the river and was soon joined by other King George Men.

One was Lieutenant William Robert Broughton. When he brought his 135-ton brig H.M.S. *Chatham*, into the Columbia River, he dubbed the small bay, where he found the *Jenny* anchored, Bakers Bay. Broughton explored the river, claiming the land and watercourse for Britain. Along the thickly wooded shore he sailed upstream past what is now Vancouver, Washington. There Broughton and his men met many Chinook and their neighbors. The Indians treated the sailors kindly, trading with them and offering them gifts of food.

On one occasion, the Chinook sent 25 canoes, carrying 150 men, to meet the British. The ambassadors invited Broughton and his men to a banquet. The sailors accepted the invitation and feasted on elk, venison, and salmon, along with roots and berries. The Indians and sailors traded goods and exchanged gifts—an ancient custom among the Chinook, who often gave presents to one another and to visitors.

Broughton's main purpose in visiting the Chinook was not trade but exploration. Without the knowledge of the large and settled Indian population, Broughton claimed the region for Britain by "right of discovery." The English used this same "right" to grant themselves license to trade in the Northwest and to build trading posts. Most Chinook welcomed traders from Britain or anywhere else, but they did not understand how the King George Men or Boston Men could lay claim to Chinook land. They would get a clearer grasp of this idea as the years passed.

After Baker and Broughton sailed away, many more ships visited the Chinook. Most traders wanted fish, furs, and clamons—suits of thick leather armor made by the Chinook and worn by their warriors. A clamon could protect its wearer from spears or arrows and was almost strong enough to prevent musket balls from penetrating the body. The Europeans did not want clamons for themselves, but for trade to other Indians farther north—including the Tlingit, Haida, and Nootka—who greatly desired them. White traders stocked up on the armor before embarking on expeditions to the lands of these other peoples.

In May 1795, Charles Bishop, captain of the *Ruby* (the *Jenny*'s sister ship) noted in his journal the importance of the trade in furs and clamons among the Chinook:

The Sea Otter skins procured here, are of an Excellent Quality and large size, but they are not in abundance and the Natives themselves set great value on them. Beaver and two or three kind of Fox Skins, Martin and River Otter are also bought here—but the best trade is the Leather War Dresses, articles to be disposed of, on other parts of the Coast, to great advantage.

White traders admired the skill of women traders. Most societies left trading to men, but Chinook women had long dealt in commerce. Chinook men did not discriminate against women; indeed, most men encouraged them. Commerce was a time-honored pursuit in the Chinook world, and it was natural that both genders should engage in it.

Chinook traders, like all people experienced at the business, liked to vary the items of exchange, especially after they had acquired a large number of certain types of goods. On one journey sea traders found that Chinook desired iron, copper, and teapots. The next time, swords, tobacco, or dentalia topped their list. Ship captains learned to pack a broad spectrum of goods—pots, pans, cloth, bells, blankets, buttons, buckets, and more. The Chinook also valued china beads and other glass baubles.

After the Chinook concluded a trading session with whites, they loaded their canoes with their goods and journeyed inland to trade with other Indians. Sometimes they traveled as far as

200 miles up the Columbia River and its tributaries, their canoes filled with iron tomahawks, metal fishhooks, bright red cloth, colored beads, and cast-iron pots. At each village they encountered, they displayed their many wares. Usually, they struck a good deal. But sometimes they resorted to an effective, though alarming, sales technique.

According to white observers, Chinook who met with resistant Indian traders pulled out guns, which they had obtained from whites, and fired them into the air. The sound and force of the blast scared the inland Indians, who knew nothing about firearms. Frightened, they were willing to agree to any deal the Chinook proposed. The Chinook would carry away plenty of goods, trade them for furs, and make a huge profit. This method of dealing worked until European traders bearing guns began to deal with inland tribes.

Once these groups became familiar with European weapons, the Chinook's noisy sales pitch lost its impact.

Many items introduced to the Chinook by European traders changed the Indians' way of life, but few changed it more than muskets, pistols, flints, powder, and lead. Indians who began to use guns for hunting and in warfare were soon at the mercy of white traders, who alone could provide manufactured weapons and ammunition. Some Indians grew so dependent on firearms that they forgot how to make and use their own weapons—spears and bows and arrows. This put them at a grave disadvantage in future trading.

Europeans introduced other harmful influences. The worst was alcohol. The Chinook had never tasted liquor until Lieutenant Broughton poured rum into fancy wineglasses and offered it to them. A few Indians downed it and soon were drunk. The unfamiliar sen-

Nineteenth-century muskets brought to the Northwest by traders employed by the British-owned Hudson's Bay Company. The Chinook used European weapons such as these for hunting and in warfare.

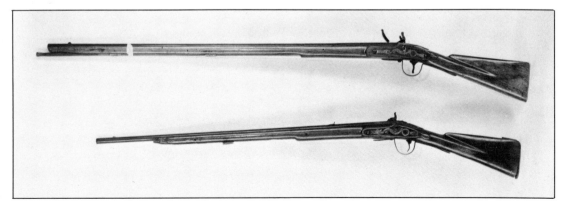

According to traditional Chinook burial practices, a corpse was placed in a canoe and surrounded by the deceased's favorite items, which sometimes included cups, pots, and weapons.

sation was so powerful that it frightened them, and they fled into the forest until they were sober. After that first scare, other Chinook tried spirits and became accustomed to their effects. Some were able to resist liquor, but others were not and became addicted to alcohol. Alcoholism quickly worsened the lives of many Chinook.

Other European diseases began to take their toll as well. The Chinook had no immunity to measles, smallpox, tuberculosis, influenza, chicken pox, and a host of other ailments introduced to them by whites. Even before the arrival

of Captain Gray, there was an epidemic among the Chinook—in 1782 and 1783, a wind carried the smallpox virus up the Columbia River. Men, women, and children broke out with skin eruptions. Ugly pustules developed all over their bodies and oozed pus.

No one knows how many Chinook died of the first smallpox epidemic, but it reduced their population considerably. Their numbers would dwindle further after they began to have closer contact with whites. Often sailors carried deadly viruses and without knowing it gave them to the Indians. The results were horrible. These diseases killed more people in North and South America than the dreaded Black Death did in Europe during the 14th century.

The Chinook also were the victims of sexually transmitted diseases, the result of sexual contact between visiting sailors and Indian women. Children born to parents stricken with venereal disease inherited the illness. Some died in infancy; others suffered blindness and other serious ailments.

These diseases defeated the efforts of the Chinook's guardian spirits and the power of their medicine people. Eventually other hardships would follow—hardships caused not by tiny germs but by human beings. But against these, too, spirit power would come up short. ▲

A page with drawings of Chinook people from the journal of American explorer Meriwether Lewis. He and fellow traveler William Clark arrived in Chinook territory in November 1804.

3

MEETING LEWIS
AND
CLARK

Trade took the Chinook far into the interior of the Northwest. Moving east, they crossed the Columbia Plateau and the Rocky Mountains and reached the Great Plains. They journeyed as far south as what is now California and as far north as present-day Alaska. But all the while they had no idea that another people, located on the eastern seaboard of North America, also planned to begin to explore this region with the intent of making it part of their nation.

These people were Americans. In 1803, the third president of the United States, Thomas Jefferson, selected Captain Meriwether Lewis and Lieutenant William Clark to lead a "Corps of Discovery" on a grand expedition across the continent. Jefferson had recently approved the purchase of an enormous mass of land, the Louisiana Territory, from the French emperor Napoléon Bo-

naparte. The American government did not know exactly where the western boundary of this territory should be established, so Lewis and Clark were sent to explore the region. Jefferson also hoped the team could trace a route along the Missouri River that reached all the way to the Pacific Ocean. The president instructed the members of the expedition to study everything they saw, including "the soil and face of the country . . . the animals . . . the remains . . . the mineral productions of every kind . . . volcanic appearances . . . climate . . . the dates at which particular plants put forth or lose their flower, or leaf, times of appearances of particular birds, reptiles or insects."

Jefferson told the explorers to treat the Indians they met "in the most friendly and conciliatory manner." The president wanted the Indians to know that Americans desired peaceful trade. Lewis and Clark were also to find out "the articles of most desireable interchange for them and us." Jefferson already knew which "article" interested him most: furs, which had already proved highly profitable to English and Spanish traders. He also instructed Lewis and Clark to search for western ports, places where American vessels could dock and traders could collect furs before shipping them to Asia.

The explorers left Washington, D.C., on July 5, 1803, and headed for the mouth of the Missouri River. In May 1804 they reached St. Louis, where the Missouri empties into the Mississippi, and then proceeded north in flatboats. They spent the winter in the villages of the Mandan Indians in what is now North Dakota. There they met Charboneau, a man who was half French and half Iroquois, and his wife, Sacajawea. The couple joined the Corps of Discovery, and Sacajawea soon had a child, whom the Americans called Pomp.

The following spring, the expedition crossed the Lemhi Pass, in the Rocky Mountains, and located the Columbia River. Lewis and Clark noted that the Indians they met there spoke some En-

Explorers Meriwether Lewis (left) and William Clark were sent by President Thomas Jefferson to explore Louisiana Territory in 1803. Their travels brought them into contact with many North American Indian tribes, including the Chinook.

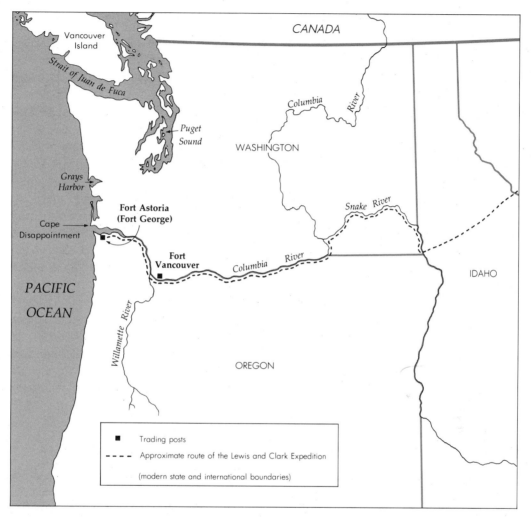

glish and wore European clothing. Obviously they had dealt with traders who must have arrived in the area by way of the Pacific Ocean. This, in turn, meant the ocean must be near. On November 7, Clark wrote in his journal that the party was "inview of the opening of the Ocian, which creates great joy." The explorers boarded canoes and traveled down the Columbia River, hugging its northern shore. All along the way, they met Chinook, who traded fish and roots for the goods brought overland by the explorers.

One day five Chinook, one dressed in a sailor's uniform, visited Lewis and Clark and traded 13 blueback salmon for metal fishhooks and other items.

The transaction went so well that Clark and most of the expedition members set up camp at Chinook Village while Lewis and a small group pressed on westward to the Pacific. Clark and his men stayed on friendly terms with the Chinook, but Lewis reported that on his expedition to Cape Disappointment he lost two rifles to Indian thieves. From that time forward, the explorers remained on their guard.

Even honest trading could be confusing. On one occasion Lewis offered an Indian two blankets for a fine sea-otter pelt. The Chinook was indignant; he said he would not give up so precious a pelt for even five blankets. His admiring eye fell on a blue-beaded belt that belonged to Sacajawea, and finally he accepted it as fair trade for his fur. The belt then passed from person to person until it landed in the hands of a woman who gave it back to members of the expedition in exchange for some blue cloth. Sacajawea thus got back her belt—and held on to the sea-otter fur.

In late November 1805, seven Clatsop—Chinook Indians who lived on the south side of the Columbia River—visited the explorers. They traded with Lewis and Clark and, in the course of their dealings, befriended them. At one point Clark offered one of the Indians a coin, a handkerchief, red beads, and a pocket watch for two sea-otter furs. The Indian refused this offer; only "Chief Beads" would do. On the Pacific coast, these beautiful blue beads were the most coveted of all manufactured beads. Lewis and Clark immediately re-

gretted that they had brought none along.

During their trading sessions, the Clatsop learned that the white men planned to spend the winter near the coast. The Indians, eager to continue trading with the whites, urged them to set up camp on the south side of the Columbia, near the Clatsop's own villages. They told the explorers that large herds of elk roamed the nearby hills, that salt was available in rich supply, and that the climate was more hospitable than it was up north. The Clatsop also claimed that their villages would afford the explorers an ideal view of the ocean. Lewis and Clark wanted to watch for ships that could take them back to the East Coast, because they were not eager to make the arduous return trip overland. The Clatsop's arguments persuaded the explorers to agree to move south.

Thus, the explorers crossed the Columbia and traveled southwest. They came upon a river in present-day Oregon that whites would later call the Lewis and Clark River and proceeded to follow it south. At a spot 200 yards from the river's bank they set up camp. There they found an abandoned Indian house, removed its posts and planks, and began to build a cluster of seven cabins, which they named Fort Clatsop. They also set up stores of food.

Lewis and Clark had few items left to trade with the Indians and needed more supplies for themselves. The men ate about three elk a day. They also fished. Fruits and vegetables, including wappatoes, small potatolike roots that were delicious and nutritious, came through trade. Whites coveted wappatoes, berries, and salmon, and the Indians demanded valuable goods for them.

Three days before Christmas in 1805, the expedition members completed the buildings of Fort Clatsop. Each cabin included a fireplace and had wood floors and bunks. During the construction, the whites were visited by *(continued on page 45)*

A 20th-century reconstruction of Fort Clatsop, a cluster of seven cabins built by the members of the Lewis and Clark expedition. The group spent the winter of 1806 among the Clatsop Indians.

LEWIS AND CLARK
AMONG THE CHINOOK

In the spring of 1804, a group of explorers led by Meriwether Lewis and William Clark left St. Louis, Missouri, and headed west. They had been appointed by President Thomas Jefferson to explore the newly purchased Louisiana Territory and to search for a river route across North America to the Pacific Ocean. Throughout their journey, Lewis and Clark kept a detailed record of the environments, the wildlife, and the peoples that they encountered. Lewis and Clark reached the Pacific Northwest in the fall of 1806 and spent the next several months among the Indian tribes of the region. The journal excerpt below was written during their stay among the Chinook and Clatsop Indians.

Wednesday, March 19th, 1806

The *Kilamox, Clatsops, Chinnooks, Cathlahmahs, Waukiacum, and Chiltz* I.[ndians] resemble each other as well in their persons and [D]ress as in their habits and manners. . . . [T]he most remarkable trate in their phisiognamy is the peculiar flatness and width of the forehead which they artificially obtain by compressing the head between two boards while in the state of infancy, and from which it never afterwards perfectly recovers. . . . I have observed the head of maney infants after this singular bandage has been dismissed, or about the age of 11 or 12 months, that were not more than two inches thich about the upper part of the forehead and reather thinner still higher. [F]rom the top of the head to the extremity of the nose is one streight line. [T]his is done in order to give a greater width to the forehead, which they much admire. This process seams to be continued longer with their female than their male children, and neither appear to suffer any pain from the operation.

The dress of the men . . . consists of a small robe, which reaches about as low as the middle of the [thigh] and is attatched with a small string across the breast and is at pleasure turned from side to side as they may have an occasion to disencumber the right or left arm from the robe entirely, or when

A mid-19th century engraving of a Chinook woman and her child. The woman's face and body are decorated with tattoos, and she wears several strings of beads around her neck.

they have occasion for both hands, the fixture of the robe is in front with it's corner loosly hanging over their arms. . . . Their robes are made most commonly of the skins of a small animal which I have supposed was the brown Mungo [probably a ferret] tho' they have also a number of the skins of the tiger cat, some of those of the Elk which are used principally on their war excursions, others of the skins of Deer, panthor, Bear, and the Speckled Loon, and blankets wove with the fingers of the wool of the native sheep. . . . [T]hey are very fond of the dress of the whites, which they ware in a similare manner when they can obtain them, except the shoe . . . which I have never seen worn by any of them. [T]hey call us *pah-shish-e-ooks* or *cloath men*. The dress of the women consists of a roab, tissue, and sometimes when the weather is uncommonly cold, a vest.

Those people sometimes mark themselves by puntureing and introducing a colouring matter. Such of them as do mark themselves in this manner prefur the legs and arms on which they imprint parallel lines of dots either longitudinally or circularly. [T]he women more frequently than the men mark themselves in this manner. The favorite orniments of both sexes are the common coarse blue and white beads as before described of the Chinnooks. [T]hose beads the men wear tightly wound around their wrists and ankles maney times untill they obtain the width of three or four inches. [T]hey also wear them in large rolls loosly around the neck, or [hanging] from the cartelage of the nose or the rims of the ears which are purforated in different places round the extremities for the purpose. [T]he women wear them in a similar manner except in the nose which they never purforate.

The men of those nations partake of much more of the domestic drudgery than I had at first supposed. [T]hey collect and prepare all the fuel, make the fires, cook for the strangers who visit them, and assist in cleaning and prepareing the fish. [T]hey also build their houses, construct their canoes, and make all their wooden untensils. [T]he peculiar province of the woman seams to be to collect roots and manufacture various articles which are prepared of rushes, flags, cedar bark, bear grass or way tape [spruce tree roots], also dress and manufacture the [h]ats & robes for common use. [T]he management of the canoe for various purposes seams to be a duty common to both sexes, as are many other occupations which with most Indian nations devolve exclusively on the womin. [T]heir feasts of which they are very fond are always prepared and served by the men.

(continued from page 41)

various groups of Indians. Clark often entertained them by firing his rifle at ducks and geese, animals the explorers then cooked and ate. When important chiefs visited Fort Clatsop, Lewis and Clark gave them gifts of tobacco and peace medals. Otherwise, the two groups bartered for goods and held out for the best deal.

One time, Clatsop chief Coboway arrived at the fort, and Lewis and Clark presented him with a peace medal. One side bore the likeness of a president—either George Washington or Thomas Jefferson. On the other was an image of a tomahawk and a pipe and an inscription: "Peace and Friendship." The explorers awarded a similar medal to Chief Taucum, one of the most important chiefs in the entire region. The whites and Indians shared a meal, smoked tobacco, and parted on friendly terms.

Two days before New Year's Day, 1806, the explorers finished building a wooden wall and gate around Fort Clatsop. Not completely trusting their Indian acquaintances, they thereafter ordered their Chinook and Clatsop visitors to leave the fort at nightfall. Many Indians objected to this inhospitable treatment—the fort, after all, sat on their land—but the explorers enforced it rigidly. Even Chief Taucum had to obey it. Lewis and Clark tried to make amends by stepping up trade.

During the winter of 1806, Lewis and Clark traded with Indian bargainers. Lewis once offered his watch, several beads, and two knives for a small sea-otter fur of rather poor quality. The Indian mistakenly thought Lewis desperately wanted the pelt and demanded twice the number of beads Lewis had originally offered. The explorer refused, and the trade ended.

The Chinook trader was surprised, and the next day he returned, this time offering to trade the same pelt for only a few strands of beads, settling for much less than Lewis had first offered. In his journal, Lewis remarked that the Chinook would do anything to make a deal. At first they sought the best deal possible, but if refused, they often lowered their sights drastically. Lewis found this a consistent "trait" among the Chinook and the Clatsop, one that emerged "from an avaricious[,] all [-] grasping disposition." In this respect, they differed "from all Indians [Lewis] ever became acquainted with."

On February 22, 1806—George Washington's birthday—a party of Indians surprised Lewis and Clark with generous gifts, including hats made of cedar bark and grass. The hats made by the Clatsop and Chinook were highly coveted. They shielded the wearer's head from rain and were beautifully decorated with woven geometric designs and dramatic scenes of Indians on a whale hunt, riding in canoes, harpoons in hand.

One day, when Lewis and Clark were at Fort Clatsop, a 105-foot whale washed ashore about 50 miles to the south, near a Tillamook Indian village.

An 1857 engraving of Northwest Coast Indians processing a whale carcass. The Indians of the region highly prized whale meat, blubber, and bone for their own use and for trade.

Clark, Sacajawea, and several men traveled to the village to get a glimpse of the giant mammal. But by the time they arrived, the whale had been cut into huge slabs.

The Indians used every part of the whale. The Tillamook placed the slabs of meat into huge wooden containers of oil along with heated rocks. They then ate the tender meat of the whale and shared it with their visitors. As the meat cooked, a sticky mass of oil and blubber formed that came from the bladder and intestines of the whale. They left the animal's bones to bleach in the sun before using them to make fishhooks or jewelry. Indians prized the items they obtained from whales and traded them at high prices.

As soon as Lewis and Clark settled in at Fort Clatsop, they began planning their return trip to the east. They dried meat and vegetables, made clothing and moccasins, and purchased canoes. It was a long journey and required much preparation. But at least the explorers now knew the route and the Indians who lived along the way. With the Indians' help, Lewis and Clark expected their return trek to be much quicker and easier than their westward journey had been. They left the Pacific Northwest and headed off for the United States on March 23, 1806.

During the previous century, the Chinook had dealt with traders who crossed the ocean; now they had been influenced by those who ventured into their country from the east by land. But this was only the beginning of contact between the Chinook and American travelers. The reports of the Lewis and Clark expedition popularized the Northwest and announced to the world that business opportunities awaited those who journeyed to meet the Chinook and their neighbors.

Lewis and Clark opened the Northwest to other traders. Even more important, the Corps of Discovery encouraged the permanent settlement of the area by whites. It did not happen immediately. Fur traders, who rarely put down roots, would dominate the scene for some years to come. Still, foreigners came to Chinook lands in growing numbers after the pioneering journey of Lewis and Clark. The Chinook had no idea of the destiny that awaited them. ▲

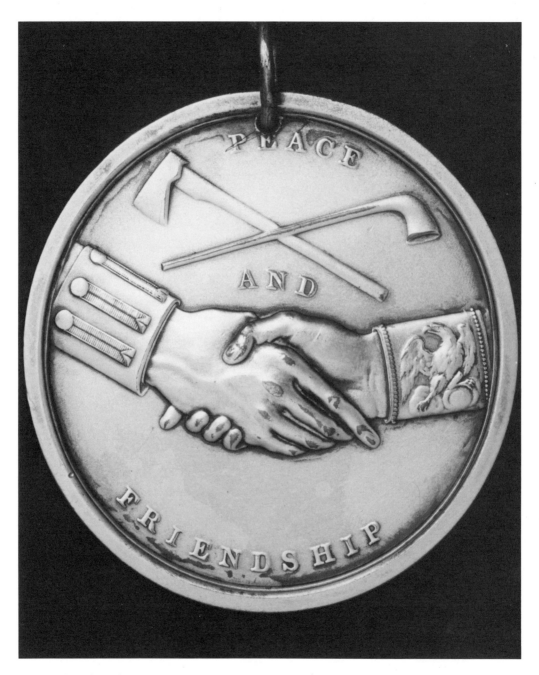

A replica of a peace medal given to Indian leaders by representatives of the U.S. government. Lewis and Clark presented such a medal to Chinook leader Comcomly in 1805.

4

CHIEF COMCOMLY
AND THE
ASTORIANS

Within the Chinook's villages and in surrounding areas, their chiefs were dominant figures. A few attained enormous prestige. One such leader stood out for his long record of dealing with white traders—Chief Comcomly, who ruled much of the lower Columbia River region. His influence was so great that whites and Indians alike called him "the greatest chief upon the river."

At first glance, the Chinook leader did not seem very regal. He was short and heavyset and had only one good eye. But Captain Charles Bishop, who met Comcomly in 1796, soon discovered that he ruled with "overwhelming force." If someone questioned his authority, Comcomly would point to a rock and announce, "As long as that rock remains in place no one shall question the power of me or of my people."

When Captain Bishop first landed in the Northwest, he invited Comcomly aboard his vessel and presented him with a suit of clothing. Comcomly, in turn, gave the Englishman gifts of venison, clamons, and bows and arrows. Before long, such displays of diplomacy had made all the white traders in the area hold the chief in high regard. As a representative of the Chinook, Comcomly became an effective leader and trader in his dealings with British, Americans, and Russians. His reputation reached Lewis and Clark, who, while encamped at Chinook Village on the north side of the Columbia River in 1805, presented Comcomly with a peace medal and probably an American flag.

The chief appointed himself the unofficial ambassador of the Chinook.

Whenever a new trading ship arrived, he took the opportunity to greet it. In 1806, for example, Comcomly canoed out into Bakers Bay to greet Captain Samuel Hill and his crewmen aboard the *Lydia*. Not long afterward, the chief sent some of his men to greet the *Derby* and its captain, Benjamin Swift. In every case, Comcomly himself welcomed the seamen and also traded with them.

These actions earned Comcomly the admiration of white traders and gave him unique power as a trader. It was he who often introduced new goods to Chinook barterers after first obtaining them from whites. One such item, molasses, soon became one of the products most sought by Indians.

Comcomly recognized that his influence with white traders would not always endear him to other Indians. In fact, some Chinook and many members of neighboring tribes envied Comcomly. But the chief seemed to enjoy being the focus of intertribal politics and usually gained the upper hand in any disputes with those jealous of his position. One reason was that he had inside knowledge about the movement of traders in the lower Columbia River region. His informants kept him abreast of most foreign expeditions into the area.

One newcomer, Nathan Winship, piloted a ship named the *Albatross* into the Columbia River on May 26, 1810. An Indian helped him sound the Columbia as he carefully steered the ship up the dangerous river. This Indian—

perhaps a Chinook trader—informed Comcomly of Winship's mission. The white man had traveled to the Columbia with 25 Hawaiians, whom the Indians called Owhyhees. They intended to establish the first permanent non-Indian settlement on the river. Winship also wanted to build a trading post, known in those days as a factory. Some Indians opposed a white presence in Indian country, but not Comcomly. He was delighted by the arrival of the whites and the boon they would bring to trade.

Winship selected a spot for his settlement on the south side of the Columbia River in what is now Oregon. It was in a low meadow, filled with oaks and cottonwoods, about 40 miles inland from the Pacific Ocean. Many Indians came there to trade salmon, roots, and furs.

All went well until a flood forced the men to reconsider their settlement site. After much discussion, they decided to move it inland. When the Chinook, Clatsop, and Chehalis—who lived to the northeast—learned that Winship planned to relocate upriver, they became upset. The Chinook tightly regulated inland trade and did not want whites interfering with it. Armed with bows, arrows, and muskets, they piled into canoes and surrounded the *Albatross* and the trading post. They told Winship that if he wanted to move the factory, he should reestablish it downstream, closer to the ocean.

The traders moved their wives and children to safety and continued to dismantle the post. Chinook warriors remained in the area, but they did not prevent the traders from boarding the ship. Winship then informed the Indians that the traders would not rebuild the post inland but instead planned to leave the Columbia River region permanently. The Chinook found this agreeable and decided to resume trade with the sailors.

Winship sailed down to Bakers Bay, where a Russian vessel, the *Mercury*, was anchored. Winship learned that its crew was being held hostage by coastal Indians. The sailors of the *Albatross* captured eight Chinook. Winship told the Indians that if they wanted their men returned, they must swap them for the Russians.

Comcomly ordered some of his men to travel north to negotiate the purchase of the Russians from their Indian captors. The men learned that the white hostages had already been released and returned to Comcomly with this news. As an act of goodwill, Comcomly offered Winship a 17-year-old Aleut Indian whom the Chinook had captured earlier as a slave. Winship accepted the young man and paid the king handsomely for him with 25 blankets and some tobacco. The chief explained that he knew of other Russian prisoners held by Indians far to the north but that it was beyond his power to order their release. Winship then let several of his Chinook hostages go free, but he did not release the rest until the day he set out down the Columbia toward the Pacific Ocean.

A 1911 photograph of a Chinook man, Kanachele Háo. His name reflects his descent from a group of Hawaiians who accompanied American trader Nathan Winship to Chinook territory in 1810. The group established the first permanent non-Indian settlement there.

Winship had learned some important facts about the Chinook. For example, he realized that many Indians wanted white traders to live among them. He also learned that the Chinook controlled the flow of commerce to and from the lower Columbia River. Ac-

An 1850 sketch of a Chinook trading canoe. The sail, however, was an innovation introduced by non-Indian traders.

cording to William Gale, an assistant to Winship, the Chinook were "in the habit of purchasing skins from the upper tribes and reselling them to the ships." Thus, Comcomly opposed factories "being established so far up" the Columbia. This would have injured Chinook trade, and, as Gale noted, the Chinook were "no doubt determined to prevent it if possible." Other traders would eventually challenge Comcomly and his neighbors for the right to trade in this part of the Pacific Northwest.

In April 1811, a violent storm struck Bakers Bay. Duncan McDougall and David Stuart, members of the Pacific Fur Company, a new trading outfit, canoed into the Columbia River in search of their ship, the *Tonquin*. The raging winds and swollen waves of the river tossed them into the churning water. Luckily, Chief Comcomly had watched the inexperienced white men foolishly brave the river during the storm and trailed behind with a pair of Chinook canoes.

Comcomly's men fished McDougall and Stuart out of the water just before they would have drowned and then took them to Chinook Village. There the Indians stripped off their drenched clothing, gave them dry garments, and fed them. The men stayed in the village for three days, resting and recovering. In gratitude, they gave gifts to their hosts. When the storm died, Comcomly returned the men to their ship. A friendship had begun.

McDougall and Stuart worked for John Jacob Astor, the millionaire owner of the American Fur Company, who had dispatched the *Tonquin* to the Columbia River to establish a Pacific post. The rescued traders described the venture to Comcomly, who was pleased to learn that the "Astorians" planned a trading post near Chinook country. The traders selected a site on the south side of the river, six miles across from Chinook Point. They went to work building the first permanent factory on the Columbia River.

Comcomly and other Chinook visited the site often. They traded with the white men as they worked on constructing the buildings that would become known as Fort Astoria. The white men had mixed feelings about Comcomly. The American author Washington Irving, in his 1836 book *Astoria*, praised Comcomly as an astute businessman and a shrewd politician. Some whites, however, worried that the chief would cause trouble.

Soon after arriving, the Astorians learned that the Chinook controlled all trade in the region. They also found out that Comcomly had traveled up the Columbia for several miles in a large canoe and told the inland Indians not to visit the white men's post. He frightened them by saying the Astorians planned to enslave Indians and sell them into bondage. Other white men had done this, so the interior Indians believed the chief.

When the Astorians learned about Comcomly's visit upstream, they were furious. They had not come to the Co-

American millionaire John Jacob Astor amassed a fortune in the fur trade during the early 1800s. He established Fort Astoria, one of the first trading posts in the Chinook's homeland.

lumbia River in search of slaves. Still, some of the traders understood Comcomly's position. The number of sea otters in the lower Columbia had declined, and Comcomly had grown dependent on the inland trade in land-animal furs, particularly beaver furs. For this reason, he struck a bargain with the Indians up the Columbia. If they traded their furs with the Chinook, they would be allowed to trap, fish, and hunt in Comcomly's territory.

Eventually, the traders broke Comcomly's hold on the inland trade by sending their own men into the inland Northwest. The traders could then deal directly with the tribes there for furs and horses. For years Comcomly had been the middleman, bringing goods from the coast and swapping them for items provided by inland people. But as the Astorians moved inland, these tribes no longer needed the chief's services. Comcomly objected to the Astorians' expeditions but was powerless to stop the traders.

Despite Comcomly's deceit, the traders learned to like him. Their sus-

An engraving of Fort Astoria as it appeared in 1813. The Astorians, as the traders there came to be known, had a fruitful trade relationship with the Chinook.

picion of the chief faded the more they knew him, but other matters clouded the relationship between the Indians and whites. Once, not long after McDougall had presented Comcomly and one of his sons with a complete suit of clothes, a Chinook stole some tobacco from the white man. McDougall decided to take up the matter with Comcomly. The next time the chief arrived at Fort Astoria, McDougall sought to impress the chief by carelessly waving a loaded gun. As he did so, the weapon exploded and a bullet tore off a piece of Comcomly's clothes. The chief raced from the fort, calling for his warriors. Armed braves arrived, prepared for a fight. Believing that Comcomly had tried to shoot McDougall, the Astorians grabbed their weapons as well. Bloodshed was prevented only because McDougall and Alexander Ross, a clerk at Fort Astoria, placed themselves between the two hostile parties and calmed them.

But the tensions had not ended. Comcomly left Fort Astoria wondering if McDougall had planned to take his life, and the Astorians began to suspect Comcomly of planning to form an Indian confederacy that would destroy their trading post. Neither suspicion was founded. The white man had shot Comcomly by accident, and the chief was not organizing an attack against the Astorians. Gradually during the winter, both sides came to their senses, and a new era of friendship dawned in the spring of 1812.

When the spring trading season opened, Comcomly learned that the Astorians had set their own prices for goods. The standard of value was the beaver fur. For instance, a Chinook could buy five twisted leaves of tobacco for one beaver fur, a hatchet or large knife for two, and a yard of long cloth or a small ax known today as a Hudson's Bay ax for four. Every trading session began with the Indians and the traders smoking tobacco provided by the Astorians. If a Chinook trader had no pipe, the Astorians gave him or her one at no cost. These courtesies were amply repaid by the Chinook, who offered the Astorians delicious fresh foods, including cranberries, oysters, and salmon. Trader Robert Stuart wrote in his journal that the Chinook salmon was "by far the finest fish I ever beheld."

At the same time that spring trade began between the Astorians and the Chinook, some white traders headed inland. Some traded with the Spokane, Okanogan, Palouse, Nez Percé, and other tribes that lived on the Columbia Plateau. Others traveled south to trade with the people of present-day Oregon's Willamette Valley.

As in the past, Comcomly was disturbed to see the Astorians chip away at his trade monopoly. He aired his displeasure to other Indians, and his words soon got back to Fort Astoria.

Once again, relations grew strained between the Indians and whites. They worsened when the Astorians learned

(continued on page 59)

CHINOOK JARGON

Chinook Jargon was a language created and used by Indian and non-Indian traders in the Pacific Northwest for hundreds of years. The jargon had a limited vocabulary of only a few hundred words, but it enabled traders from many nations to communicate and conduct business successfully with one another.

Chinook Jargon was probably originated by the Chinook and the Nootka. These two Indian groups lived near one another and had a strong trade relationship, but they did not share a common language. For trade negotiations, the Chinook and the Nootka had to learn a few words from each other's language, which became the jargon's core.

Beginning in the late 18th century, French, Russian, English, and American traders began to explore the Pacific Northwest. These foreigners learned to speak the jargon as well. They soon added new groups of words and sounds from their own languages because they offered items, such as glass beads and alcohol, that the Indians had never seen before and for which they had no words in their own languages.

In the mid-19th century, at the peak of its use, Chinook Jargon may have been spoken by as many as 100,000 people. Its speakers included most of the Northwest Coast Indians and almost all of the settlers in what are now Oregon and Washington, and British Columbia, Canada. Chinook Jargon fell into disuse only when, in the 1870s, American settlers began to outnumber greatly the Indian inhabitants of the region. As a result, English soon replaced the jargon as the language of trade.

However, for many years Chinook Jargon had enabled people from many different cultures to communicate with one another—no small feat. It served this purpose so well in part because it was easy to learn. The jargon's vocabulary was always small. Instead of adding more and more words over time, jargon speakers discarded any words that were no longer needed in negotiations. The most commonly used jargon words expressed uncomplicated ideas in the simplest way possible. If jargon speakers wanted to express any shade of meaning, they had to rely on gestures or changes in the pitch of their voice.

Ca-po', n. (E). (French,-Capot). A coat.

Cha'-ko, chah'-ko, or chahco, v. (N). Nootka, clayoquot,—chako; Tokwaht,—tchokwa). To come; to approach; to be or become. "In this latter sense it forms the passive voice in connection with many other words. Often it is joined with adjectives and nouns, and forms other verbs. **Yaka chako pahtlum**, he is drunk; **nika chako keekwulee**,—I am degraded; **yaka chako stone**,—it is petrified. Perhaps more properly the word in this connection to become, than to be, at least it is often so, as in the latter example the meaning would also be,—to become stone; **chako rotten**,—is to become rotten. Occasionally too the passive voice is shown by placing the word **iskum** before the main word, as, **yaka iskum kow**,—he is arrested."—Eells. Ex.: **Nika chako kopa Poteland**,—I came from Portland. **Kloshe mika hyak chako**,—good you come quick. **Chuck chako**,—the tide is rising—(literally, is coming). **Chuck chako pe klatawa**,—the tides. **Halo chako**,—to linger. **Wake kunjih yaka chako halo**,—Indelible,—(literally,—never will it become gone). **Chako Boston**,—to become an American; often said of Indians who are becoming civilized like white people. **Chako delate**,—to become right, true, or good. **Chako delate till**,—to become exhausted. **Chako hyas tum tum**,—to become proud. **Chako huloima**,—to vary; to become different. **Chako kah nika nanitch**,—to appear. **Chako kloshe tumtum**,—to love; to reform; to become friendly; to get a good heart. **Chako kloshe**,—to get well; to become good. **Chako kunamokst**,—to congregate; assemble; convene; meet; unite; join. **Chako mimolouse**,—to die; to become rotten; to become decayed (as potatoes or vegetables). **Chako pahtlum**,—to become drunk. **Chako skookum**,—to become strong, especially after a sickness, to show complete recovery. **Chako soleks**,—to become angry; to quarrel. **Chako pelton**,—to become foolish; to be cheated. **Chako waum tumtum**,—to be earnest; to become excited. **Chako youtl tumtum**,—to become glad; to be glad. **Chako polaklie**,—to become dark; night is coming. **Chako oleman**,—to become old. **Chako halo**,—to be destroyed; to disappear; to vanish; to be all gone. **Chako elip hiyu**,—to exceed. **Chako kunamokst nika**,—come with me.

Chee, adv., adj. (C). (Chinook,-t'shi). Lately; just now; new; fresh; original; recent. Example: **Chee nika ko**,—I have just arrived. **Hyas chee**,—entirely new, very new. **Chee chako**,—a new comer; just arrived. **Delate chee**,—entirely new. **Klootchman yaka chee malieh**,—a bride.

Chik'-a-min, n., adj. (N). (Tokwaht,-

tsikamen;Nootka,—sickaminny (Jewitt); seekemaile,—(Cook). Iron; metal; metallic; steel; money; cash; mineral. Example: **T'kope chikamin**, (white metal), silver. **Pil chikamin**, or **chikamin pil** (yellow metal),—gold or copper. **Chikamin lope**,—wire; a chain. **Nika hyas tikegh chikamin**.—I very much wish money. **Illahee kah chikamin mitlite**,—mines.

Chik'-chik, (**Tsik'-tsik**, or **Tchik'-tchik**), n. (J). By onoma. A wagon; a cart; a wheel; any wheeled vehicle. Example: **Tsiktsik wayhut**,—a wagonroad. **Nika chako kopa chikchik**,—I came in a wagon. **Piah chikchik**,—railroad cars. **Lolo kopa chikchik**,—to haul in a wagon.

Chinook—*(Chinook Indians). These Indians formerly lived near the mouth of the Columbia river, where the Chinook Jargon language was mainly developed in its formative period, and hence more words were adopted into it from that language than any other Indian language, and so its name was given to the language. Properly speaking the Chinook language means the old Chinook, and the Chinook Jargon the language described in this dictionary; but the old Chinook is about obsolete, and for the save of brevity, Chinook wawa means in common conversation the Chinook Jargon, while the proper language of the Chinook tribe is called the Old Chinook. The Chinook land and Chinook Indians have, however, reference to the tribe as it formerly existed.—Eells.

Chinook wind. The Chinook is always a strong, steady southerly wind, never from any other point of the compass, unless it be slightly southwesterly. It is distinctly peculiar to the Northwest Pacific coast and its source is far out in the nasty storm center of the Pacific ocean, emanating from the famed Japan current, which is the source of the remarkable humidity of the North Pacific coast.

Chinook canim,—the large canoe used on Puget Sound. **Chinook illahee**,—the land of the Chinook Indians. **Chinook tillikums**,—the Chinook Indians. **Chinook wawa**,—the Chinook language. Example: **Mika kumtux Chinook wawa?** Do you understand the Chinook language?

Chitsh, n. (S). (Chehalis,-tshitsh). A grandmother. (Gibbs, Gill, Hibben, St. Onge and Swan, give chope for grandfather; but Hale and Tate give the meaning as grandfather and chope as grandmother. Eells says "I never heard either word used on Puget Sound." Eells gives the following: Ex.: Grandmother, —mama yaka mama; grandmama: nitz. Papa yaka papa,—grandfather. Tenas yaka tenas klootchman,—granddaughter. Tenas yaka tenas man,—grandson. Te-

A page from George C. Shaw's 1909 book The Chinook Jargon and How to Use It. *The jargon, which was used by both Indian and non-Indian traders to conduct business, was a mixture of English, Chinook, Nootka, Russian, and several other languages.*

Below are several examples of how speakers of Chinook Jargon combined several words from different languages to communicate an idea. Underneath the phonetic spelling of each jargon word is its English translation and an abbreviation that designates its language of origin (c = Chinook, n = Nootka, s = Salish, e = English, f = French, u = origin uncertain).

United States	BOS'-TON American (e)*	IL'-LA'-HEE country (c)		
president	TY-EE' boss (n)	KO'-PA in (c)**	WASH'-ING-TON Washington (e)	
hair	TUP'-SO grass (c)	KO'-PA on (c)	LA-TA-TE' the head (f)	
thunder	SKOOK'-UM great (s)	NOISE noise (e)	KO'-PA in (c)	SAG'-HA-LIE sky (c)
trout	TZUM spotted (c)	SAM'-MON salmon (e)		
Bible	SAG'-HA-LIE sky (c)	TY-EE' boss (n)	YA'KA his (c)	BOOK book (e)
drunkard	PAHT'-LUM full rum (c, e)	MAN man (e)		
beloved	KLO-SHE good (n)	KO'-PA in (c)	TUM'-TUM heart (u)***	

* "Boston" came to mean "American" in the jargon because the first American ships to reach Chinook country sailed from that city.
** Kopa is one of the few prepositions in Chinook Jargon. Among its possible meanings are *to, around, about, in, into,* and *onto.*
*** This word is possibly an imitation of the sound of a heartbeat.

(continued from page 55)

that their ship, the *Tonquin*, had suddenly exploded near Vancouver Island, claiming the lives of several Astorians and leaving their fort undermanned. McDougall feared Comcomly might take advantage of this misfortune to launch an attack.

McDougall called a council with the Indians. He brandished before them a small bottle and said it was filled with smallpox. If the Indians threatened war, McDougall promised to uncork the death-filled bottle. The Indians were persuaded to remain friendly and nicknamed McDougall the Great Smallpox Chief.

McDougall's fears were not justified. True, Comcomly and other Chinook leaders could have summoned enough warriors to exterminate the Astorians. But the chiefs wanted to continue trading with them. Indeed, Comcomly was so intent on improving relations with the whites that in the fall of 1812 he allowed his son to accompany an Astorian, Gabriel Franchère, on an excursion up the Columbia River. Comcomly's son introduced Franchère to many inland Indians and helped him trade for food and furs. He also taught Franchère the Chinook Jargon.

Another event brought the Indians and whites even closer together. That winter, one of Comcomly's daughters, Illchee (which means "Moon Girl"), and McDougall fell in love. In accordance with Chinook tradition, McDougall sent two representatives—who were clerks at Fort Astor—to visit Chief Comcomly. On behalf of their boss,

they asked the chief for his daughter's hand in marriage. Comcomly agreed, and after an exchange of gifts, the two parties settled on a dowry.

On July 20, 1813, Comcomly prepared for Moon Girl's wedding day. He donned a fine red breechcloth and a bright blue blanket and adorned his body with colorful paints and feathers. Moon Girl joined her father and the family for a long canoe ride across the Columbia River to Fort Astoria. The wedding party included many grand canoes.

When they reached the south side of the Columbia, traders were waiting with horses for the royal family. They rode to the fort, where the Indians and whites exchanged many gifts, including beads, axes, knives, cloth, and kettles. Everyone then sat down to a large feast. After the celebration, the couple made their home at Fort Astoria.

This bond proved mutually beneficial to the Astorians and the Chinook. McDougall received the loyalty of Comcomly's family, who gave him the choicest trade items along with valuable information about Indian trade, wars, and alliances. For his part, Comcomly received special treatment at the fort. The blacksmith, for instance, gave him many useful tools and trade goods made from iron and copper.

As the Chinook and the Astorians cemented their alliance, relations between the United States and England fell apart. In January 1813, Donald McKenzie, an Astorian trader who dealt with inland Indians, learned from Brit-

An 1857 engraving of non-Indian fur traders hunting sea otter. The piece appeared in The Northwest Coast, *a book by James G. Swan, an American who spent three years in the region.*

ish trappers employed by the North West Company—a fur-trading company based in Montreal, Canada—that war had broken out between England and the United States. It was the War of 1812, and soon the fur traders were drawn into it.

Traders from the North West Company visited Astoria, and in October 1813 they purchased the fort. The next month, Comcomly visited McDougall and reported to his son-in-law that a ship seemed ready to enter the Columbia River. Comcomly assumed it was a British ship and urged the Astorians to do battle with its crew. According to Alexander Ross, the chief explained that there were only a "few King George people who come down the river; they were poor; they have no goods, and were almost starving; yet you were afraid of them [the British]."

Comcomly then told the Astorians that he had "eight hundred warriors, and we will not allow them [the British] to enslave you. The Americans are our friends and allies." McDougall thanked the chief for his concern but explained that the North West Company now owned the fort. The white man asked Comcomly to lay aside his weapons and leather clamons. He also asked the chief to find out if the ship indeed belonged to the British.

The ship proved to be the *Raccoon*, a British naval vessel armed with 26 guns. It anchored in Bakers Bay, and Comcomly, heading a force of canoes, paddled out to visit the captain and crew. He greeted them as he had greeted so many seamen in the past. He swore allegiance now to the British and promised complete friendship and trade. Comcomly gave the *Raccoon*'s captain a fine sea-otter fur and in return received a complete naval uniform. The captain also presented Comcomly with a British flag.

The next day Comcomly canoed across the Columbia. He wore his new uniform and the flag fluttered over his head. Later he attended a ceremony that transferred Fort Astoria into British hands. The chief watched the traders run the British flag up the pole at the fort and the *Raccoon*'s captain break a bottle of wine on the flagstaff. The post was then officially renamed Fort George. But despite the new name and the new faces there, Comcomly in the years to come would remain a welcome visitor to the post as he and his people became regular trading partners with the British. ▲

A trade token with the image of a beaver on it used by traders employed by the North West Company, which purchased the fort at Astoria in 1830. Traders used tokens to represent trade items during the exchange of goods with Indians.

5

THE ERA
OF THE
KING GEORGE MEN

After the British took control of Fort Astoria in the fall of 1813, Chief Comcomly tried to maintain good relations with the traders there. He liked dealing with the British as well as the special privileges they gave him. The British seemed to be of two minds about the Chinook chief, however. Some described him in glowing terms in their journals. Others called him a "troublesome beggar," "niggardly fellow," or "mercenary brute."

The reason for these contrasting views was that Comcomly had more on his mind than pleasing outsiders, especially when they brought woe to the Chinook. It disturbed him, for instance, that white traders had introduced alcohol to his people. Drinking had harmed many Chinook families, including Comcomly's own. He never touched spirits himself, but on one occasion, one of his sons got drunk at Fort George. When he stumbled back to his village, everyone—including the slaves—laughed at him, and Comcomly was humiliated.

Another time, one of Comcomly's sons became so intoxicated that he foamed at the mouth, babbled, and repeatedly fell to the ground. Certain his son had gone mad, Comcomly suggested that someone shoot him, but fortunately the chief's suggestion was not followed. Shaken by these experiences, Comcomly wisely discouraged the liquor trade, but he was powerless to prevent the British from selling spirits or the Chinook from consuming them.

Alcohol was only one of the chief's concerns. He learned that the British were thinking of moving their trading post inland to Cowlitz Indian country, which was about 100 miles east of the Chinook homeland. Such a move would deprive the Chinook of valuable trade, so he spread word that he would retaliate if the Cowlitz began dealing with the British.

In this way and in others, Comcomly wielded enormous power, and traders at the North West Company began to resent it. They particularly objected to the special treatment that Comcomly received from ship captains. For instance, in March 1814, the *Pedlar* entered the mouth of the river, and the ship's captain showered Comcomly with gifts—including a red military coat, white shirt, pants, socks, and shoes—when the chief canoed out to greet the ship. The captain then treated Comcomly and one of his sons to a delightful dinner. Comcomly received similar treatment when the *Isaac Todd*, the supply ship of the North West Company, entered the Columbia River in 1814. The chief enjoyed being invited aboard, but not as much as other Chinook did.

One Chinook who welcomed the friendship of the North West Company was Ramsey, the expert navigator who piloted the *Isaac Todd* across the bar and into the river. He had guided ships many times before and would repeat the favor often in the future. In return, Ramsey received good payment and much recognition from the British.

Another Chinook who was especially pleased with his visit aboard the *Isaac Todd* was a son of Comcomly's.

The young man fell in love with one of the ship's passengers, a woman named Jane Barnes. She had blond hair and blue eyes and captured the heart of many Chinook. Comcomly's son was so taken with her that he made a marriage proposal that included an extravagant dowry of 100 sea-otter furs. Jane Barnes gently refused the offer and soon sailed away, never to return.

More than once, traders were nonplussed by the traditional Chinook greeting and did not know how to respond. For instance, when the *Columbia* entered the river, two of Comcomly's sons, Casacas and Selechel, canoed out to trade with the ship. But the sight of strange Indians approaching frightened the inexperienced white sailors, who loaded the ship's 10 cannons and prepared for a fight. Tensions calmed, however, and two days later, Comcomly, his wives, and the other members of his family were permitted to board the ship to trade salmon and sturgeon.

The traders at Fort George grumbled about Comcomly's friendly relations with the crews of incoming ships. They objected especially loudly to his close relationship with Americans. The War of 1812, which had ended in 1815, had left the United States and England on uneasy terms. In 1818 the King George Men learned, to their outrage, that Americans had returned to Chinook country to claim the region for the United States. That year, when Captain James Biddle sailed into the Columbia River at the helm of the *Ontario*, a vessel

(continued on page 73)

CRAFTS OF THE COLUMBIA

The rich environment of the Pacific Northwest's Columbia River region traditionally provided the Chinook Indians with everything they needed. The Indians used some of these resources to make beautiful, as well as functional, objects for their everyday use. Such pieces included carved bowls and utensils from wood and animal horn, and woven baskets and clothing from grass and rushes.

The Chinook embellished their everyday items with abstract and lifelike decorative designs. The most common consisted of rows of parallel lines that were carved or woven in wave or sawtooth patterns. They also exaggerated or altered human and animal shapes, balancing the decorated and undecorated areas of their images. All designs were created to conform to and enhance the form of the object.

Chinook crafts were an integral part of their society and, as such, said much about their way of life. Indeed, the amount of decoration often indicated the social position of the owner. Highly decorated objects belonged only to those who could afford them; pieces with little embellishment were owned by the lower classes. Thus, the Chinook's crafts reflected the social system of the tribe.

A 9½-inch wooden fishhook handle decorated with a carved wolf effigy, made in the early 20th century. Chinook men attached hooks to the narrow end of such handles and used them to pull large fish from the water.

A mid-19th-century hair comb topped with an effigy of a human face. This face resembles those carved on the masks that members of many Northwest Coast tribes wore during ceremonies.

An early-20th-century wooden bowl carved in the shape of a bear, about 4½ inches long and 2 inches wide.

A wooden bowl, about 7 inches in diameter, collected in the late 19th century by American ethnologist George Gibbs from the Northwest Coast's Shoalwater Bay area.

A bowl made from a mountain sheep's horn. The piece is about 8 inches in diameter and is decorated with geometric engravings.

A female figure with child, about 7½ inches high, carved from an elk antler.

A horn bowl, 7½ inches in diameter, engraved with human faces and geometric patterns. The Chinook steamed or boiled the horns to make them easier to carve.

An early-20th-century horn ladle. The handle is carved into the shape of a bird's head.

A basket adorned with black animal
shapes and geometric patterns.

Chinook women made baskets from vegetable materials that grew in their lands. They most often used the roots and bark from spruce and cedar trees, and rushes found along the banks of rivers. The baskets shown here were made in the early 20th century using the twining method. The basket maker first formed the basket's skeleton by bending several spruce- or cedar-root ropes into the shape of a U. She then wove ropes horizontally in and out of these to create the basket's sides. Twined baskets were often so tightly woven that they could hold water without leaking.

A basket with spruce-root handles.

A cedar bark openwork basket.

A basket decorated with interwoven black fibers.

71

A twined basket and lid, woven in the early 20th century.

A flat basketry bag made from rushes.

(continued from page 64)

equipped with 20 cannons, the British feared an alliance had been made between the United States and the Chinook. One had not, but the arrival of the Americans did signal a change. The United States soon renewed its efforts to claim portions of the Northwest. Ultimately it would succeed.

For the time being, however, the main contest within the region involved competing Indian factions. Chinook villages were often at odds with one another or with neighboring Indians as each sought to do business with foreign traders.

Among the Chinook's greatest adversaries were the Cowlitz. The root of their disagreements was trade: The Chinook wanted to control the inland trade with the Cowlitz, who, in turn, wanted to ignore their enterprising neighbors.

In 1818, Chief How How of the Cowlitz visited Fort George with the hope of establishing peaceful trade with the whites. The traders were delighted by his visit and even suggested that one of their men marry one of the chief's daughters.

The Chinook did not take kindly to this, and while the wedding arrangements were being made, a Chinook fired a gun at How How in an attempt to assassinate him. Thinking that How How had shot at them, the traders in confusion fired their cannons at the Cowlitz, wounding one of them. How How immediately sent his most trusted slave to find the guilty Chinook. The slave tracked the culprit down and stabbed him to death with a dagger.

Chinook guide and navigator Ramsey. This image was published in 1845 in Narrative of the U.S. Exploring Expedition *by naval lieutenant Charles Wilkes, who led a group of explorers through the Chinook's territory in 1841.*

The conflict between the Chinook and the Cowlitz gradually cooled, but the Chinook's relationship with another group, the Clatsop, grew more heated. Over the years, the two peoples had shared many things, including a common language. But contact with whites had divided them, and tensions mounted. A pivotal incident occurred in 1825 when two of Comcomly's sons—Selechel (also known as the Duke of York) and Duke of Clarence—became gravely and mysteriously ill. After local medicine men failed to help them, the chief appealed to a Clatsop healer. The doctor tried his best, but his cures did not help the young men, who grew worse by the hour and finally

Sea captain James Biddle, who in 1818 came to Chinook territory aboard the Ontario. *He was one of the first U.S. traders to attempt to reclaim the Northwest from the British.*

died. In his grief, Comcomly blamed the Clatsop medicine man and sent a slave to kill him. The healer's murder enraged the Clatsop, and both groups—who lived on opposite sides of the Columbia River—prepared for war.

The Clatsop gathered at Fort George to hold a war dance. No fewer than 50 warriors assembled. Shouting war threats and firing their rifles in the air, they then marched in unison from the fort to the beach. At the beach they formed a circle and continued to dance, yelling every two or three minutes.

The warriors wore clamons made of thick elk skin and covered their bodies with red, black, and yellow paint. Many

shook war rattles made of shells. They were also heavily armed. Some brandished rifles and pistols; others wielded bows and arrows. Those with knives took wild swipes at the air. Like all soldiers about to take the field, the Clatsop braves whipped themselves into a hostile mood.

Despite these preparations, the Clatsop and the Chinook did not fight a pitched battle. Even so, a wedge had been driven between these longtime friends. Without intending to do so, the white traders had pitted the Chinook against the Clatsop. As the years passed, their differences grew.

A turning point came in 1821 when the North West Company merged with its biggest competitor, the Hudson's Bay Company. The merger marked the beginning of great changes in trade in the region, and Indians on both sides of the Columbia worried about their fate. The situation remained uncertain until George Simpson, superintendent of the Hudson's Bay Company, arrived to survey the area. After only a short time on the river he decided the company's headquarters must be moved, in part because the Chinook dominated all trade near the Pacific Ocean.

Simpson correctly reported to his colleagues that the Chinook were "keen traders." This did not bother him, but he voiced concern that "through their hands nearly the whole of our Furs pass." Comcomly and the Chinook were "so tenacious" that they had created a "monopoly." Simpson argued that the Chinook were so jealous of their trade that they would stop at nothing to hold on to their grip. They told other Indians that whites were "Cannibals, and every thing that is bad in order to deter them from visiting the Fort." The Chinook eagerly encouraged marriages between their daughters and influential Indians or whites as a means of extending their power over trade. Simpson believed the Chinook would willingly murder the British if it would strengthen their control on commerce. Consequently, the superintendent concluded that the Chinook posed a serious economic threat to white traders. He felt the only answer was to relocate the Hudson's Bay Company headquarters upriver.

Comcomly learned of Simpson's plan on March 16, 1824, when the superintendent crossed the Columbia River to announce his intentions directly to the Chinook chief. Simpson explained his plan as the two men strolled along the banks of the river, and Comcomly wept at the news. Not only would the chief lose control of the Indian trade in the region, he would lose his friends at Fort George. Both prospects upset him.

Three days later, the traders christened Fort Vancouver, at a place known to the Chinook as Skitsotoho. It was an ideal location for a trading post. There the riverbank sloped down to the Columbia River, affording the traders a grand view of the landscape. To the south was the Willamette River, which formed a fertile valley that was soon to be inhabited by white settlers. To the

The Hudson's Bay Company coat of arms. In 1821, the British company merged with the North West Company and took control of Fort George.

north was Puget Sound, another future site of white settlement.

Without white traders nearby, life would never again be the same for the Chinook. Comcomly's influence waned and passed to Chief Casino, whose village was located near Fort Vancouver.

Casino was no stranger to Comcomly. In fact, Comcomly had been the upstart's father-in-law since 1817, when the white trader McDougall left the region. Moon Girl—McDougall's wife and Comcomly's daughter—stayed behind and married Chief Casino. But the marriage did not quiet the feud over commerce that developed between the two chiefs. At one point Casino tried to block Comcomly's canoes from traveling upriver to Fort Vancouver. Dr. John McLoughlin, the chief broker at the

Hudson's Bay post, calmed the situation. Eventually, he persuaded the two men to accept a truce that kept the river open to all trade.

This era of change caused other difficulties for Chief Comcomly. In 1825 he lost eight members of his family. In addition to the two sons whom the Clatsop healer had failed to cure, six others died of disease and were buried along the sandy beach between Point Ellice and Chinook Point. These deaths, painful as they were, only hinted at the greater losses Comcomly's people would soon suffer at the hands of unseen enemies.

In 1827 and 1829, Comcomly greeted an American trading vessel, the *Owhyhee*, commanded by John Dominis. The Chinook traded fish and furs for muskets, lead, powder, blankets, beads, red and blue cloth, and liquor. In 1829, as Dominis piloted the ship into the Columbia, he marked the channel with buoys. A Chinook took one of the floating markers back to his village. Before he arrived back at his home, he felt strange. He soon began to tremble and complained of being cold.

When the ailing man arrived home, the villagers built a great fire and covered him with fur blankets. Still, his teeth chattered. The Indians destroyed the buoy, but the man died. Another epidemic had come. It would soon carry many more Indians to the afterlife, "Land Beyond the Sea." Few Indians doubted that the disease was brought by whites, some of whom also died,

although not in as large numbers as the Chinook.

The Chinook called the new disease the "Cold Sick." Some whites believed it was malaria or ague. Most likely, it was influenza. The sailors were exposed to the flu in distant ports, particularly in Asia, where a deadly virus had developed. For Indians, who had no immunity to the flu, the results were disastrous. Hall J. Kelley, a Boston schoolmaster who visited the Chinook in 1834 and later wrote about the epidemic, reported that when he arrived at the mouth of the Columbia River, he saw little except "darkness and blackness and desolation" and "heard but little more than the sighs and cries of the misery in the perishing remnants of the Clotsop and Chenook tribes, and the roar and rage of mighty waters." The toll was so great that there were not enough survivors to bury the dead. Bodies were simply laid in heaps. Birds picked at the corpses, and the bones were left to bleach on the beaches.

Between 1830 and 1840, the Chinook population declined by nearly two-thirds. Flu accounted for a large number of deaths, but a smallpox epidemic in 1836 also claimed many lives. The diseases affected the Chinook living along the Columbia and at Shoalwater Bay. Men, women, and children watched helplessly as pustules formed on their bodies. Those infected sickened and died quickly. "The aspect of things is very melancholy. . . . Scarcely one of the original race is now to be seen," wrote one observer. So many Chinook died at Shoalwater Bay that their enemies felt emboldened to move into the region. During the 1830s, the Chehalis took over portions of the area.

The Clatsop suffered as much as their Chinook neighbors. Many retreated to a village at Point Adams where Chief Kotata watched over the remnants of his tribe.

Some whites interpreted the epidemic as a sign of a divine plan by which God meant to extinguish the Indians. "The aboriginal inhabitants of America shall make way for another race of man," said one Christian. Others held that "the Great Dispenser of human events" had decided to reduce the Indian population "to mere shadows of their former greatness." God, in sum, was "removing the chief obstruction to the entrance of civilization, and opening a way for the introduction of Christianity where ignorance and idolatry had reigned uncontrolled for many years."

An 1845 drawing of the Hudson's Bay Company trading headquarters at Fort Vancouver. The British established the fort about 80 miles southeast of Chinook territory, thereby cutting off the Indians' control of trade in the region.

In 1835—in the middle of the Cold Sick epidemic—Chief Comcomly was struck by the disease and died. The chief's family cleaned Comcomly's body and dressed him in his finest clothes. Other Chinook placed him in a large canoe that served as his coffin. They paid homage to him by surrounding his body with many valued items, including shoes, cups, kettles, and weapons.

Hudson's Bay Company's chief broker, Dr. John McLoughlin. He kept peace among the Indian tribes vying for control of Northwest trade.

Originally, Comcomly's relatives placed the canoe in the family cemetery at Point Ellice. For several months, the Chinook mourned his death. Then another tragedy struck. One night, Dr. Meredith Gairdner, a white man, robbed Comcomly's grave. He cut off the chief's head and, like a ghoul, ran off with it and other parts of the chief's body. The family was outraged, and there was talk of retaliation. Instead, the Chinook moved the body to a secret spot safe from other grave robbers. Most Chinook were not sure where it was concealed, though some elders claimed it lay in the forest behind Fort George.

Dr. Gairdner claimed he stole Comcomly's head for "scientific" reasons. He sent the head to Britain so that scientists could study the skull—a fashionable practice at the time. The Chinook were repulsed by it and believed the spirit world took great offense at such thefts. Not long after Dr. Gairdner robbed Comcomly's grave, he died of tuberculosis. The Chinook claimed that the doctor had been punished for his misdeed.

The Chinook and their friends demanded the return of Comcomly's skull. Finally, in 1972, more than 100 years after it was stolen, the British returned it to the United States. The Chinook people buried it in the Ilwaco Community Cemetery in southwestern Washington, where it remains today.

The tomb of Chinook chief Comcomly. He died in 1830 from a disease—probably influenza—brought to Chinook country by non-Indians.

According to Chinook oral tradition, his spirit became a star, planted high in the heavens.

With the passing of Comcomly came the passing of an era. The chief's position fell to his brother Chenamus, who ruled from the village of Qwatsamuts on Bakers Bay. But after the epidemics of the 1830s, things would never be the same for the Chinook. Life had changed forever at Shoalwater Bay and on the Columbia River. ▲

Stum-manu, also known as William Brooks, a Chinook follower of Methodist missionary Jason Lee. Stum-manu traveled with a non-Indian missionary group to the East Coast to solicit financial support for the Chinook.

6

COPING
WITH
INTRUDERS

During the early 19th century, Chief Chenamus continued Comcomly's old practice of greeting trading vessels that traveled down the Columbia River. In 1839, the chief and his wife, Sally, canoed out into Bakers Bay to visit and trade with the crew of the *Sulphur*, a British naval vessel assigned to sound and chart the Columbia. One member of the team, assistant surgeon Richard B. Hinds, described the Chinook royalty in glowing terms. He found Chenamus "a sedate, discreet, dignified man" and Sally "a very useful character" because she supplied him with many trade goods.

Hinds became so friendly with Sally that she invited him to her village, which was located at the mouth of the Wallicut River. "Whatever may be said derogatory to these people," Dr. Hinds wrote, "inhospitality is not among the number of their failings." The surgeon was received cordially and led on a tour of the village. Sally even took Hinds to the family cemetery and pointed out two fresh graves. One held Chenamus's son; the other, the young man's bride. Both were probably victims of disease.

Sally also gave Dr. Hinds a tour of her large cedar home. The surgeon marveled at the beautiful dwelling, particularly the platform where Chief Chenamus sat. It had a backdrop of painted designs and stood against a wall decorated with colorful circular patterns. A giant wooden figure, carved from cedar and painted in red and black, protected the area from bad medicine power.

Just as many Christians believe in the spiritual power of the crucifix, so the Chinook believed in the spiritual power of certain sculptures and wooden objects. They further believed that all things—animate and inanimate—had power. Some Europeans and white Americans balked at this notion and called the Chinook "savages" and "heathens." Others were even persuaded that Indians were children of Satan and must be rescued from his evil hands.

The Chinook religion, like that of most Indians, distressed whites so deeply that many sought to "save" the Indians—that is, to convert them to Christianity. On May 21, 1840, the *Lausanne* anchored in Bakers Bay. Its passengers were missionaries from the Methodist Episcopal church who hoped to make Christians of the Indians living in the Columbia River valley. On the same day, Father Modeste Demers, a Catholic priest with the same goal, landed across the bay in Astoria.

Chenamus and Sally, on separate visits to the *Lausanne*, were surprised to learn that its crew had brought no rum. They were equally surprised to learn that the missionaries planned to abolish slavery among the Chinook. If the people freed their slaves, the Chinook wondered who would get the wood and water and catch salmon.

On May 22, Father Demers canoed across the Columbia River to meet the Chinook. He had made extensive preparations for this occasion. For the better part of a year, he had composed a dictionary of Chinook Jargon. He also had translated catechisms, prayers, and hymns into the trade language. By the time he appeared among the Chinook, he knew the jargon well enough to communicate with the Indians.

Demers spent three weeks with the Chinook, "instructing the adults, baptizing the children and doing much good." He then left the region, but several years later another priest, Father J. Lionnet, arrived in Chinook country to continue Demers's work. Between 1847 and 1852, Lionnet operated a mission among the Chinook on the north shore of the Columbia River. Unlike Demers, Lionnet made no advance preparations. He was mystified by the Chinook language, which he called "gibberish." And he did not know how to deal with the harsher aspects of their lives, such as the violence that erupted over trade or alcohol, the fatal diseases, and gambling, a popular Chinook pastime. Nevertheless, Lionnet felt he had made some headway. In a letter, he observed, "My savages begin to communicate with the grace. . . . God," he added, "has put his arms around them and their frightened course is opening to the light of the truth."

Over the years, however, Lionnet became discouraged. He wrote that the "savages are few in number and several of them who remain are now traveling so that there are only small numbers to whom I teach the catechism." By 1852, he had concluded that his teachings and efforts had made no impression on the Chinook, who preferred to live their own lives without the intervention of the priest. Lionnet told his superiors that the Chinook were "hard headed" and left the mission in defeat.

Things went just as badly for the Methodists who arrived in the Northwest in 1840. After resting at Fort Vancouver, they received their assignments. Reverends John H. Frost and Daniel Lee were told to minister to the Chinook and the Chehalis, and they joyously accepted the challenge.

Frost and Lee traveled downstream to Astoria and began to prepare for their first meeting with the Chinook. On July 13, 1840, they crossed the Columbia River. As soon as they encountered Indians, the missionaries explained that from now on the Chinook must obey certain rules. First of all, they were to stop trading for anything but food. Next, they were to learn to pray to the "Great Christian Chief."

The Chinook treated Frost and Lee cordially, as they always treated whites, and politely ignored their strange demands. The next day, the two mission-

Old Mission House, Willamette Valley, *an 1841 sketch by American artist Joseph Drayton. Many Christian missions were established in Chinook territory, but few of the Indians there were converted .*

aries, thoroughly deflated, returned to Astoria. One day among the Chinook convinced the missionaries that they should instead establish their mission among the Clatsop. But if Frost and Lee believed that the Clatsop would embrace Christianity with enthusiasm, they were sorely mistaken.

Back in Astoria, Frost learned that one Clatsop had recently killed another. To avenge this murder, a Clatsop man slaughtered a woman and cut her body to pieces. A feud began and soon raged out of control. At Pillar Rock on the eastern end of the Columbia River, a group of Indians killed Kenneth McKay, a white man, and his Indian friend. James Biernie, a trader at Fort George, feared more violence and sent messengers to Fort Vancouver and to the Chinook's villages asking for help.

Chief Chenamus acted quickly. He boarded a canoe and traveled across the river accompanied by about twenty warriors. They began to search for the men who had killed McKay. Meanwhile, Chief Squamaqui, a Kathlamet chief who rivaled Chenamus for power, rounded up two suspects, an Indian from the Quinault tribe to the north and a slave. After Squamaqui left, the Quinault escaped but was recaptured by Squamaqui, who handed him over to Dr. John McLoughlin, a trader at Fort Vancouver. McLoughlin ordered his men to hang the Quinault, and soon after his execution the killing south of the Columbia ended.

Chenamus returned to his home, and Frost began his missionary en-deavors among the Clatsop. The minister moved to Clatsop Plain, a site that, according to Frost's journal, was considered "a wild region" filled with "ignorant, superstitious and barbarous" Indians. Again, Frost failed. The only Indians interested in hearing the gospel were a chief named Kotata, his wives, and their slaves.

Like Lionnet, Frost did not know how to communicate with the Indians he hoped to convert. He found the Chinook language "so defective, that thereby it is impossible to acquaint them with the nature of the law." In fact, the Chinook language was very complex, probably too complex for Frost to learn. In addition, what Frost had to say hardly stirred the Indians. Even when his message came through loud and clear, both the Chinook and the Clatsop shut their ears to it.

Frost and Lionnet failed to convert the Chinook to Christianity. But they did help usher certain changes into the Indians' lives, most of which were detrimental to them. But the harm caused by the missionaries was only a part of the greater destruction of Indian cultures that was brought on by the influx of white settlers into the Northwest in the mid-19th century.

From 1830 to 1850, the Chinook population declined dramatically, mainly because of disease. During the same time, more white traders and pioneers began to arrive. From 1842 to 1847 some 7,000 new settlers came to present-day Oregon, swelling the non-Indian population that already included many traders. In 1851, the Chinook in the area numbered only 171; the Clatsop, only 80. But in what is now Clatsop County in Washington State alone, there were 462 whites, 249 of them in Astoria.

Steadily, the U.S. government made its presence felt in the area. In 1848, Astoria became an official port of entry to the region, boasting a U.S. customshouse. Soon after, the federal government surveyed the Washington and Oregon coasts and built a lighthouse at Cape Disappointment. Most important, in 1849 the United States formally established Oregon Territory and named Joseph Lane the first territorial governor and superintendent of Indian affairs.

The arrival of representatives of the American government spelled doom for the Chinook. In 1849 the United States added the Department of the Interior to its many agencies in Washington, D.C. The Bureau of Indian Affairs (BIA), which had been founded in 1824 as part of the War Department to supervise the government's dealings with Indians, was assigned to the new department.

The BIA officials who came to Chinook territory wanted to enforce there Indian policies that had already been put into action elsewhere in the country. The intention of these policies was to open Indian lands to white settlement. The federal government could do this, however, only after it had secured ownership of this territory by negotiating treaties with the Indians who inhabited it. Governor Lane proposed to

The U.S. government established a customs house at Astoria in 1848 to foster an American presence in the Northwest. One year later, Oregon Territory was formally organized, and Astoria became an official U.S. port of entry.

buy Indian lands and to remove, or relocate, all native peoples in Oregon Territory east of the Cascade Mountains. Lane planned to establish two reservations—one on the Grande Ronde River and the other at what is now Fort Hall, Idaho—on which the removed groups would live.

Governor Lane's plans came closer to reality when the U.S. Congress passed the Donation Land Act on June 5, 1850. The bill called for three commissioners to negotiate treaties with the Indians of the Northwest. It also authorized the removal of Indians—including the Chinook and their neighbors—to the east side of the Cascades. Most important, the law encouraged whites to move into the

Joseph Lane, first governor and first super-intendent of Indian affairs for the territory of Oregon.

been appointed subagent for the Chinook and Clatsop, a position that made him responsible for overseeing the government's dealings with the Indians. He was married to a Clatsop woman and had some understanding of Indian culture. Consequently, Shortess resisted the plan to remove the Indians from their homes, fishing areas, and burial grounds. He proposed instead that the government establish a reservation for the Chinook and the Clatsop north of the Columbia River near Shoalwater Bay.

Shortess recognized the Chinook's tie to their land and the river. Wisely, he also wanted the Indians to keep their fisheries so that they would always have a source of food. If the Chinook and Clatsop secured a reservation in their own homeland, Shortess argued, it would afford them "all means of pasturage and agriculture [so] that they can be materially improved in character and condition."

The top policymakers at the BIA did not share Shortess's views. They wanted the Chinook out of the way. In frustration, Shortess wrote in 1850, "For myself, I have so long preached patience and hope to them that I am almost ashamed to do so any longer." These remarks displeased the superintendent of Indian affairs, who soon replaced Shortess.

On August 1, 1851, Anson Dart, Oregon Territory's new superintendent of Indian affairs, met with several coastal Indian groups on a broad, sandy beach at Tansey Point, eight miles down-

vacated areas. Married couples who settled there before September 1, 1850, could claim 640 acres, and a single male could claim 320 acres. After December 1851, the amount of land whites could settle was cut in half, but land was still available to them. Soon whites streamed into the Northwest.

The Indians, who were already badly outnumbered, watched their territory dwindle. They had an ally, however, in Robert Shortess. Shortess had stream from Astoria. Dart negotiated treaties with them that would transfer ownership of their territory to the United States in exchange for reservation land. The Clatsop were pressured to give up half a million acres in exchange for a small reservation at Point Adams in what is now northwestern Oregon. The reservation measured only three and one-half miles long, one mile wide at its southern end, and two miles wide at the northern end. They retained one of their ancestral burial grounds but lost many more, along with a host of sacred places and holy shrines.

The Chinook fared even worse. Dart viewed the Chinook as a vanishing people. In Dart's report to Commissioner of Indian Affairs Luke Lea, he wrote that they were once "the most powerful Nation upon the Pacific coast; now [they are] wasted to a few over three hundred souls." Believing the Chinook needed much less land than they traditionally had occupied, Dart compelled them to cede a huge number of acres north of the Columbia River. He allowed them to keep only a few parcels of land for individual homes. They retained the right to fish, cut wood, pick cranberries, and raise animals and crops on this territory only.

In return, the Chinook received $400 in cash and, for 10 years, less than $2,000 worth of annuities—yearly payments of food, clothing, cloth, tobacco, soap, rifle caps, molasses, and gunpowder. At the Chinook's demand, the government also agreed to remove a trader named Washington Hall, who dealt in alcohol from Indian territory. They won this point but few others. In the end, the United States would pay $91,300 for more than 3 million acres, a price of about 3 cents an acre.

Superintendent Dart sent the treaties to Washington, D.C., for the approval of the commissioner of Indian affairs, the head of the BIA. He forwarded the treaties to President Millard Fillmore, who read them and forwarded them to the Senate. The treaties were entered into the congressional record but were never ratified. This made no difference to white settlers and territorial officials, who acted as if the treaties were law. White settlers moved freely onto lands that still legally belonged to the Chinook and the Clatsop, and for the Indians matters only got worse. ▲

A Chinook woman carrying a traditional basket, photographed in 1910 by Edward S. Curtis.

DECLINE
AND
REBIRTH

After Superintendent of Indian Affairs Anson Dart met with the Chinook in 1851 at Tansey Point, he recorded his thoughts in a report to the commissioner of Indian affairs. The Chinook, he wrote, "are fully aware of the rapidity with which, as a people, they are wasting away." They also recognized "the power of the Government." But they did not accept that they could "be killed and exterminated."

The Chinook made it clear to the superintendent that under no circumstances would they "be driven far from the homes and graves of their fathers." This belief was tested in the years that followed. For even though the Senate failed to ratify Dart's treaties, white settlers poured into the Oregon Territory.

It soon became evident that a new treaty must be negotiated with the Chinook, approved by the Senate, and signed into law by the president. The prospects for this improved in 1853 when President Millard Fillmore created Washington Territory by splitting Oregon Territory into two political divisions. He appointed Isaac I. Stevens to serve as the first territorial governor and superintendent of Indian affairs for Washington.

This land division separated the Chinook from the Clatsop. The Chinook now lived in Washington Territory, and the Clatsop lived in Oregon Territory. In 1853, Stevens appointed William H. Tappan as the Chinook's agent and ordered him to conduct a census of the group. Tappan counted 126 Chinooks living on the Columbia and 70 Chinook-Chehalis living on Shoalwater Bay. Then another smallpox epidemic broke out. A second census—done in 1854—tallied 79 Chinooks north of the Columbia River. The government evidently did not bother counting heads at Shoalwater Bay another time.

As soon as Governor Stevens arrived in Washington Territory, he began negotiating treaties with the Indians there. In 1854 and 1855 he met with representatives of many groups at Medicine Creek, Point Elliott, and Point-No-Point. He then instructed Tappan to gather the Indians of southwestern Washington for a council. When Tappan visited the Chinook to invite them, he received a cold reception. Tappan wrote Stevens that the Indians were bitter about mistreatment by agents and believed Tappan's words were as "unavailing as the wind that blows."

On February 25, 1855, Governor Stevens held the council on the Chehalis River, about 10 miles upstream from the point where the river enters Grays Harbor. Some Chinook attended as part of a total group of some 850 Indians representing various tribes, including the Quinault, Chehalis, Satsop, and Cowlitz. The representatives wore their best clothes, painted their bodies, and adorned themselves with beads.

Governor Stevens addressed them in English. A translator, Benjamin Franklin Shaw, repeated his words in the Chinook Jargon. The Indians themselves then translated these words into their own languages. It was a laborious process, especially when the complex legal terms of the different treaties had to be explained. But the gist of Stevens's remarks was plain enough: He asked all the Indians represented at the council to move to one large reservation that would be established in the land that stretched north from Grays Harbor to Cape Flattery.

In return for giving up their native lands, the Chinook and the others would receive payments. Stevens offered them $40,000 in annuities and $400 to clear the lands for farming. In addition, the treaty called for teachers, blacksmiths, carpenters, and doctors to live among the tribes. Slavery and alcohol would not be permitted on the reservation. The Chinook were not impressed by this arrangement. Shrewd bargainers, they knew that they were actually receiving much less than they were giving.

Chief Narchotta, who represented the Chinook from Shoalwater Bay, politely heard Stevens out before responding. According to James Swan, an early white settler at Shoalwater Bay, Chief Narchotta opened his remarks on a cordial note. He said that when the conference began the Indians "did not understand you; it was all dark to us as the night; but now our hearts are enlightened, and what you say is clear to us as the sun." It was now clear, he continued, that the whites wanted the Chinook to desert their homes and their sacred burials. But this was not acceptable. "Our fathers, and mothers, and ancestors are buried there," Chief Narchotta explained. He said that the Chinook wished to continue burying their dead in these sacred spots "and be buried [there] ourselves." They wanted "to have a place on our own land where we can live, and you may have the rest; but we can't go to the north among the other tribes." He pointed out that the various tribes were "not friends, and that if we went together we should fight, and soon we would all be killed."

Thus, the Chinook were not inclined to sign Stevens's treaty. They were even less so when a young Chehalis chief, Tleyuk, spoke up and explained to the governor that he wanted to secure for his people a reservation in his own land. Stevens replied that the U.S. government did not recognize Tleyuk as a chief.

Tleyuk then declared that the Chehalis would have nothing to do with a treaty. He, the other Chehalis present at the council, and the Chinook all left the treaty grounds on March 3. No treaty resulted from this conference, and once again the Chinook were left without a legal document defining their lands. Because the Chinook reached no formal agreement with the United States, the government would not recognize the Chinook as a tribe, a situation that would harm the Indians for years to come.

Four months after this council, special Indian agent Michael Simmons succeeded in negotiating a treaty with the Quinault and several smaller tribes living to the north of the Chinook. The

Isaac I. Stevens was Washington Territory's first governor and first superintendent of Indian affairs. He negotiated treaties with most of the Indians in the region.

treaty resulted in the formation of the Quinault Reservation at the mouth of the Quinault River. Over time, some Chinook and Chehalis from Shoalwater Bay moved onto portions of this land.

In late 1855, the Clatsop also agreed to a treaty following a meeting with Joel Palmer, the Oregon superintendent of Indian affairs. The superintendent forwarded the treaty to the president, who

Joel Palmer, who replaced Joseph Lane as Oregon's superintendent of Indian affairs. He set down the terms of a treaty between the United States and the Clatsop, but the document was never ratified by Congress.

then sent it to Congress. But, once again, the Senate did not ratify the treaty, and the Clatsop were left without a formal agreement with the United States. However, on November 9, 1855, President Franklin Pierce issued an executive order that created the Coast Range Indian Reservation in northwestern Oregon, and some Clatsop moved there.

When Stevens and Palmer completed their treaty councils with the Indians west of the Cascade Mountains, they trained their sights inland—on the large and powerful tribes living in eastern Oregon and Washington. Some of these tribes met with Stevens and Palmer at the Walla Walla Council of 1855, and three treaties were negotiated.

But the tribes who had been pressured to sign the agreements at this council grew increasingly dissatisfied with the treaties' terms. Three months later, the tension escalated into violence as the Indians clashed with settlers and soldiers. Some groups from the coast and Puget Sound were drawn into the conflict. In 1856 the Plateau Indians approached the Chinook living along the lower Columbia River and at Shoalwater Bay and tried to enlist them in the battle. The Chinook elders pointed out that their people were few in number and ill prepared for war. They had few guns and little powder and lead. Also, the battles were being fought far away, in the Puget Sound region and in the interior. Few Chinook agreed to fight.

Most settlers were not surprised that the Chinook remained peaceful. The newcomers shared the sentiment of a white man who wrote in 1856 that he felt "no particular fears from the war, or any of the Indians, unless it is that they wont bring us half salmon enough." By the 1850s the Chinook Indians were in no position to threaten whites. Chinook men and women understood this, and so did most of the white population.

In 1864, Thomas J. McKenny, Washington superintendent of Indian affairs, proposed moving the nontreaty Chinook onto the newly created Chehalis Reservation. He offered the Chinook many inducements, including holding a potlatch—a ceremonial feast at which government officials would be expected, as the hosts, to present many gifts to their Chinook guests. But the Chinook were not interested in leaving their homes at any price.

In September 1866, the government finally set aside 355 acres on the north shore of Shoalwater Bay for the Chinook and established the Shoalwater Bay Indian Reservation; between 30 and 40 Chinook and Chehalis families already lived on this land. Some of them had homes both on this reservation and on the Quinault Reservation.

The Clatsop on the Coast Range Indian Reservation were less fortunate. A year earlier, the government seized the middle portion of the reservation and renamed the northern part the Siletz Indian Reservation and the southern part the Alsea Indian Reservation. Some of the Clatsop who had lived on the Coast Range Indian Reservation remained on these two small ones, and more tribe members came to join them. Others stayed on the south shore of the Columbia River. Legally, the Clatsop lost all their lands. But because the Clatsop were not perceived as a threat to white settlers, they were left alone.

Throughout the last half of the 19th century, the main concern of the Chinook was survival. More and more whites flooded into their area. Many pushed north, beyond the Columbia River area. Others moved onto the shores of Shoalwater Bay. Whites and Indians soon began to compete for the right to fish in these waters.

Whites at Shoalwater Bay were flourishing in the oyster business. During the 1850s and 1860s, white businesses fished about 30,000 bushels of oysters from the bay each year and made approximately $100,000 annually from the oyster trade. Some Chinook also worked in the trade, but usually as employees of white-owned companies. Those Indians who did continue to work independently ultimately sold most of their catch to whites.

The Chinook also found other livelihoods. Some picked cranberries from the purple bogs that dotted the region. Some hunted fur-bearing animals, such as the sea otter, though prices had fallen since the heyday of the fur trade. Many Chinook still fished for salmon and sturgeon in Shoalwater Bay, the

Columbia River, and other nearby waterways.

Before long, even fishing became a problem. As the demand for fish opened commercial opportunities for whites, they sought more efficient methods for netting and trapping. One innovation brought to the west coast by easterners was the fish wheel. This was a large wheel with nets attached to it that was placed on the back of fishing vessels. As the water's current rotated the wheel, the nets scooped up large quantities of fish. These devices dramatically increased profits, and the industry grew. Soon white businessmen opened salmon canneries where Chinook villages once stood. Chinook Village, Point Oak, Point Ellice, and Tansey Point all became cannery sites.

By 1880, some 40 canneries were in operation on the Columbia River and employed Chinese immigrants to slit open large numbers of fish. The inedible portions of the animals were then pushed into the Columbia River and washed out to sea. This method of handling fish was offensive to the Chinook. For centuries they had fished for salmon, a creature they viewed as sacred and worshiped in their annual salmon ceremonies. Now they were powerless to stop a major industry from depleting their homeland's rivers of salmon.

Meanwhile, settlers continued to arrive in increasing numbers. Their homes, businesses, schools, and churches sprang up on or near Chinook and Clatsop villages. Worse, the settlers showed no respect for the Indians' culture. Grave robbers plundered Chinook and Clatsop cemeteries and sold the remains, particularly skulls, to avid collectors all over the world. Sacred Indian skulls ended up as desk ornaments. Burial clothing, purses, pouches, knives, medals, and jewelry were stolen and sold as novelties. Day by day, the Chinook saw their sacred objects and ways debased.

By the end of the 19th century, it seemed that the Chinook might disappear as a people. On June 1, 1884, the San Francisco *Chronicle* lamented that the Chinook and Clatsop, "the most conspicuous coast tribes, and in all respects a superior race of aborigines," were now "among the lost tribes of Oregon." Some whites referred to the Chinook and the Clatsop as the "Vanishing Red Race."

Some scholars tried to "save" the Indians' languages and cultures. Franz Boas, an anthropologist at Columbia University in New York City, traveled to the Chinook country to study the people and their languages. He wrote two important works on the Chinook and Kathlamet for the Bureau of American Ethnology. Verne Ray continued Boas's work in his own study of Chinook culture. Years later, Robert Ruby and John Brown worked with some tribal elders and produced *The Chinook Indians: Traders of the Lower Columbia River*. It is the most comprehensive study of the Chinook, written by the two most prolific historians of northwestern Indian history.

Land claims emerged as a crucial issue for the Chinook in the late 19th and early 20th centuries. Some claims hinged on the provisions of the treaties that established the Quinault Reservation and the Shoalwater Bay Indian Reservation on which some Chinook continued to live. These treaties gave the government the right to divide these communally held reservations into small parcels of land, known as allotments. Allotments were to be owned as private property by individual Indians. The allotment process was accelerated after Congress passed the General Allotment Act of 1887 (also

A U.S. government outpost in the Upper Cascade mountains, photographed in 1867. It was the site of a violent conflict in 1856 between non-Indian settlers and Indians who were dissatisfied with the terms of treaties they had negotiated with the U.S. government.

An 1857 engraving of non-Indian oystermen on the Northwest Coast. Non-Indians took over many of the Chinook's traditional fishing sites during the 1850s and 1860s.

known as the Dawes Act, after Massachusetts representative Henry L. Dawes). This legislation allowed reservations throughout the country to be allotted.

The Chinook living on Quinault Reservation received allotments, but some of those on Shoalwater Bay Indian Reservation had difficulty convincing the government of their legal right to the land they occupied there. By the late 1920s, only three Chinook families resided permanently on the Shoalwater Bay reservation. Four children in these families had not received land allot-

ments, so in 1927, President Calvin Coolidge ordered that one be given to each of them. Unfortunately, the Chinook families did not know that the president gave this order, so they requested allotments for their children on the Quinault Reservation. When President Franklin Roosevelt took office in 1933, he consequently denied the children allotments at the Shoalwater Bay reservation. During the 1930s and 1940s, the Chinook maintained a village at Shoalwater Bay. The eight families that lived there through these years survived primarily by fishing.

Their relatives on the Columbia River never received a reservation. Some visited friends and family on the Shoalwater Bay Indian Reservation and rented lands and housing from whites. Others purchased small parcels of land. Without a treaty or a reservation, these Chinook had no legal claim to their ancestors' lands and therefore could not demand that the government return their territory, as other Indian groups across the nation had begun to do.

In the early 1900s, some of the Indians of the lower Columbia River did sue the United States, claiming their lands had been taken from them and that they had never received payment for them. In August 1912, the U.S. Court of Claims awarded several tribes small amounts of money. The Chinook received the largest award—$20,000. The Kathlamet and Wahkiakum got $7,000, and the Nucquechahwemuck $1,500.

In 1946, the U.S. government established the Indian Claims Commission to consider the land claims of various groups. But only tribes that were officially recognized by the government were permitted to make claims to the commission. Tribes could be recognized only if they had reservations or had negotiated treaties with the United States in the past. Although unrecognized, the lower Columbia River Chinook filed a claim in 1951. They sued the government for $30 million in payment for the loss of more than 762,000 acres and natural resources that had

been taken from the Chinook in the 19th century. They argued that with this land loss they had also sacrificed hunting, fishing, and gathering rights as well as lumber. The commission filed the Chinook claim under Docket 234. This meant that before the commissioners could hear the Chinook's case, they first had to determine if the Chinook—an Indian group not recognized by the federal government—could legally make such a claim.

The process was complicated because two distinct Chinook groups existed, one at Shoalwater Bay and one along the Columbia River. Still other Chinook lived on reservations also occupied by the Quinault, Chehalis, Siletz, Grande Ronde, and Tillamook. These different Chinook strands had to be woven together. In 1951, John G. Elliott and a number of other Chinook along the Columbia River organized themselves into a tribal entity, which they called the Chinook Nation. Two years later, a Chinook woman named Myrtle Woodcock organized the Indians at Shoalwater Bay into a political body with an established set of by-laws that stated their goals and the requirements for membership into the group. The Indians met and, under the terms of Washington State law, incorporated into the Chinook Indian Tribe.

The Chinook at Shoalwater Bay then elected officers. Woodcock became the secretary-treasurer, and Roland Charley and Lewis Hawkes were voted chair and vice-chair, respectively. The people elected Jack Petit, Claud Waian, Charles Larsen, and Paul Petit directors of the tribe. Soon the Chinook from the river and the bay began to cooperate on some projects to benefit both groups. Tribe leaders worked especially hard to better medical and dental health services for all Chinook and to improve education, cultural awareness, housing, and economic development in their communities.

Some years passed before the Indian Claims Commission handed down a decision on Docket 234. In November 1971 the commission decided to award the Chinook $75,000, adding that the money the Chinook had received from the U.S. Court of Claims in 1912 should be subtracted from this sum. The adjusted total came to $48,692.05—a far cry from the $30 million for which they had sued.

The members of a Chinook fishing crew, including members of Chief George Charley's family, photographed in the early 1900s. Some of the crew are holding equipment for baseball—a game introduced to them by non-Indians.

The question of Chinook claims against the United States was thus resolved. But other issues lingered. The Chinook were still not officially recognized by the government. Moreover, none of the Chinook's original land had been returned to them. Many Chinook remained homeless.

But land is only one of the many concerns of the Chinook today. They have also worked hard to revitalize their culture and community, often by spiritual means. In the 1880s a new Indian religion, called the Indian Shaker church, began at Mud Bay, Washington. In about 1900 many Chinook turned to this faith and found new hope in its combination of ancient Indian beliefs and Christianity. In the 1980s, the church continues to give strength to many Chinook.

Another example of cultural rebirth is the Chinook Heritage Project, begun in 1979 by tribal elders at Shoalwater Bay and supported by funds from the National Endowment for the Humanities, the Washington State Commission for the Humanities, and the Native American Studies Program at Washington State University. The purpose of the project was to assemble historical and cultural data on the Chinook. As part of this project, university professors and community elders formed a research team that has collected photographs and interviewed tribe members. This information now provides the basis of public programs and exhibits depicting the life and culture of the Chinook Indians.

Two Oregon State Police officers in Willamette Township remove hidden Indian fishing nets. Indians fished there illegally until 1974, when the U.S. government gave them the right to catch as much as half of the fish in the region.

The project showed that the Chinook no longer are a unified tribe but instead now form three groups. One group, the Wahkiakum Chinook, live on the Quinault Indian Reservation, where they are in the forefront of legal battles for Indian fishing rights in the Northwest. In 1974, they and other groups of western Washington Indians won a major victory with the ruling of federal court judge George H. Boldt in *United States v. State of Washington*. The ruling, known as the Boldt decision, stated that the government's past treaties with these groups gave them the right to fish in the fishing sites used by their ancestors. It also stated that the tribes were entitled to half of the fish caught by Indians and non-Indians in these areas. The Supreme Court has upheld the decision. Some Chinook were pleased by the ruling, but others felt that fishing should be conducted by Indians alone.

The second major group is the Chinook Indian Tribe, which in 1955 formally framed its constitution and won recognition from the state of Washington. Since 1970, the Chinook Indian Tribe has been an integral participant of the Small Tribes Organization of Western Washington, which fights for the rights of many non-federally recognized tribes in the state.

The third Chinook group lives at Shoalwater Bay. The Chinook here applied for federal recognition, which was granted after a lengthy process in 1979. Today they work actively to improve their health, education, and economic development. They are proud to be citizens of the United States and veterans of both world wars and the Vietnam War, but they are equally proud of their unique culture. Two Shoalwater Bay Chinook have also distinguished themselves as artists. Lynn Clark is famed for her beautiful beadwork, and Tom Anderson is renowned for his wood carvings.

George A. Charley, who died in 1935, was the last Chinook chief at Shoalwater Bay to have his head flattened according to Chinook tradition. He summed up his love of the Chinook country in a poem, whose powerful words speak for all Chinook Indians today:

> I have traveled o'er the country
> that was once our Domain seen the
> lovely Shoalwater Bay where our
> council fire would burn. Give us a
> place of trust, or honor. Let us feel
> this is still. Let us use our mind and
> muscle. Let our action be our own.

Chief Charley's dream lives on, as do the history and culture of the Chinook. Perhaps it is captured best in an ancient Indian story. According to the elders, there was once a great tribe of Chinook salmon that traveled annually up the Columbia River when spring came, led by the Salmon Chief and his wife. They guided the tribe upstream, bringing with them a warm wind off the Pacific. However, five Wolf Brothers and five North Wind Brothers hated the Chinook Chief and decided to kill him.

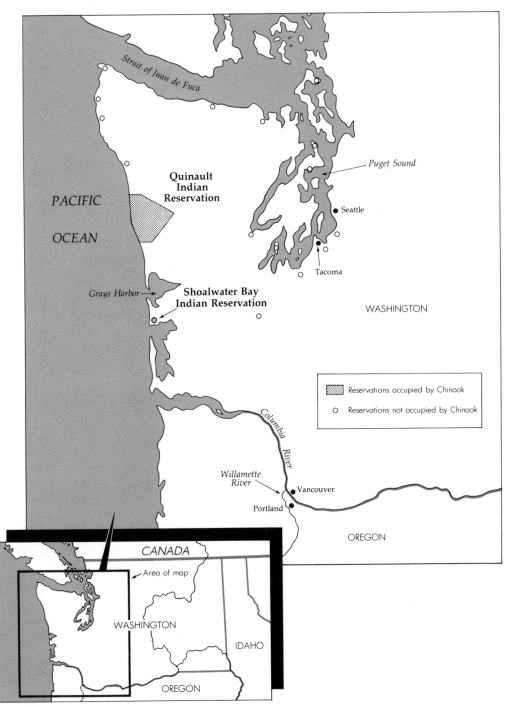

RESERVATIONS IN WESTERN WASHINGTON STATE TODAY

Chinook chief George Charley, who died in 1935, was the last tribe member to have his head flattened according to Chinook tradition.

The strong North Wind Brothers met the Salmon Chief in hand-to-hand combat. The leader of the Chinook Salmon defeated three of the North Wind Brothers. But the fourth brother threw the chief to the ground and killed him. Then, in a murderous frenzy, the North Wind Brothers and their allies destroyed all of the Chinook Salmon Tribe. They even cut open the chief's wife and killed every salmon egg in her body—every egg except one.

One of the salmon eggs became lodged in a tiny space between two large rocks. Try as they might, the North Wind Brothers could not reach this egg. They decided to leave it, believing it would dry up and die. The Creator, who witnessed all of this, then sent rain to cleanse the battleground and revive the egg. The egg washed into the sand and became a small fish. The baby Chinook salmon swam to the ocean, where it met its grandmother.

With the help of his grandmother, Young Chinook Salmon grew big and strong. His grandmother told him what had happened to his mother and father. Young Chinook decided to avenge the death of his people. When he had grown larger and stronger than his father, his grandmother sent him up the Columbia River to face the five North Wind Brothers. In hand-to-hand combat, Young Chinook met and killed all of them. The land, which had been frozen since Chinook Salmon Chief's death, began to thaw.

Like the salmon people, the Chinook were nearly destroyed. Only a

A group of young people, including two Indian girls, assist in the cleanup of an Indian cemetery on the Shoalwater Bay Indian Reservation. The burial ground's restoration is part of the Chinook's ongoing effort to honor their past.

few survived the effects of white expansion, but those few have grown strong and have dedicated themselves to the survival of their people. The Chinook look to the future as a challenge and know they can meet it. They take pride in their accomplishments and progress. But, above all, they glory in their unique heritage and in their undeniable identity as Chinook. ▲

BIBLIOGRAPHY

Boas, Franz. *Chinook Texts*. Bureau of American Ethnology Bulletin no. 20. Washington, DC, 1894.

Gibbs, George. *Tribes of Western Washington and Northwestern Oregon*. Contributions to North American Ethnology, vol. 1. Washington, DC, 1877.

Johansen, Dorothy O. *Voyage of the Columbia Around the World with John Boit, 1790–1793*. Portland, OR: Champoeg Press, 1960.

Meares, John. *Voyages Made in the Years 1788 and 1789: From China to the North West Coast of America*. J. Walter, 1791.

Ray, Verne F. *Lower Chinook Ethnographic Notes*. University of Washington Publications in Anthropology, vol. 7. Seattle: University of Washington Press, 1938.

Ross, Alexander. *The Fur Hunters*. Norman: University of Oklahoma Press, 1956.

Ruby, Robert H., and John A. Brown. *The Chinook Indians: Traders of the Lower Columbia River*. Norman: University of Oklahoma Press, 1976.

Swan, James G. *The Northwest Coast*. Fairfield, WA: Ye Galleon Press, 1966.

THE CHINOOK AT A GLANCE

TRIBE *Chinook*

CULTURE AREA *Northwest Coast*

GEOGRAPHY *Western Washington and Oregon*

CURRENT POPULATION *Approximately 1,700*

FIRST CONTACT *John Meares, British, 1788*

FEDERAL STATUS *The Chinook who reside at Shoalwater Bay Indian Reservation have been recognized by the federal government. Other Chinook have incorporated under the name Chinook Indian Tribe and have been officially recognized by the state of Washington. The Chinook who live on the Quinault Indian Reservation have not been recognized.*

GLOSSARY

aboriginal The term applied to the earliest inhabitants of a region.

agriculture Intensive cultivation of tracts of land, sometimes using draft animals and heavy plowing equipment. Agriculture requires people to live in fairly permanent settlements.

annuities Yearly payments of money, food, clothing, fabric, tobacco, and/or other items.

Boldt Decision The 1974 ruling of the federal court judge George H. Boldt in *United States v. the State of Washington*. The decision states that the U.S. government's past treaties with Indian groups in the Northwest ensure the right of their descendants to fish in traditional tribal fishing sites. It also entitles these groups to half of all the fish caught by anyone in these areas.

Bureau of Indian Affairs (BIA) A U.S. government agency now within the Department of the Interior. Originally intended to manage trade and other relations with Indians, the BIA now seeks to develop and implement programs that encourage Indians to manage their own affairs and to improve their educational opportunities and general social and economic well-being.

catechism A summary of the basic tenets of a religion in the form of questions and answers.

Chinook Jargon A specialized language used in the Pacific Northwest in the 18th and 19th centuries by both Indians and non-Indians to conduct business. The jargon was a mixture of English, Chinook, Nootka, Russian, and several other languages.

clan A multigenerational group having a shared identity, organization, and property based on belief in descent from a common ancestor.

culture The learned behavior of humans; nonbiological, socially taught activities; the way of life of a group of people.

dentalium A tubular white shell found only north of the Strait of Juan de Fuca in the Pacific Northwest. This was the principal item of currency and trade for the Chinook.

Guardian Spirit Ceremony A Chinook ritual celebrating the spirit powers that guided their life. The ceremony lasted five days, during which tribe members displayed the powers that their individual guardian spirits had bestowed on them and implemented special cures prescribed by medicine people.

head flattening A traditional Chinook practice in which an infant's head was placed in a special cradleboard that applied pressure to the front of the child's soft skull. When children were taken out of this device, their forehead was permanently sloped.

Indian Claims Commission (ICC) A U.S. government body created by an act of Congress in 1946 to hear and rule on claims brought by Indians against the United States. These claims stemmed from unfulfilled treaty terms, such as nonpayment for lands sold by the Indians.

Indian Territory An area in the south-central United States in which the U.S. government resettled Indians from other regions, especially the eastern states. In 1907, the territory became part of the state of Oklahoma.

lore Traditional beliefs and knowledge gained through experience and education and passed down through oral or written stories.

medicine man/woman A person called on by a guardian spirit to become a healer. Such tribe members were responsible for diagnosing and curing illnesses, finding missing people, and contacting the dead. Sometimes Chinook individuals would hire a medicine man or woman to cause harm through witchcraft as well.

mercenary A person who is primarily concerned with obtaining material wealth or who promotes a cause solely for economic gain.

missionaries Advocates of a particular denomination who try to convert nonbelievers to their faith.

monopoly The exclusive control of a commodity or service by one group and/or control of the region in which the commodity or service is distributed.

reservation A tract of land retained by Indians for their own occupation and use.

Suyapee The Chinook word used to describe white men. Literally meaning "upside-down face," the word originated from the Chinook's first contact with a group of whites, one of whom was bearded and bald.

territory A defined region of the United States that is not, but may become, a state. The governor of a territory is appointed by the president, but territory residents elect their own legislature.

Thunderbird The creature responsible for the Chinook's creation, according to the tribe's oral tradition.

treaty A contract negotiated between representatives of the U.S. government or another national government and one or more Indian tribes. Treaties dealt with the cessation of military action, the surrender of political independence, the establishment of boundaries, terms of land sales, and related matters.

tribe A society consisting of several or many separate communities united by kinship, culture, and language and other social institutions including clans, religious organizations, and warrior societies.

vision quest A fast and vigil undertaken by Indian youths in the hope of receiving a sign from a supernatural power who might guide and protect them throughout their life. The vigil usually required a person to stay outdoors alone, with little food, for an extended period of time.

weir A wooden fence or rock wall constructed in a stream to trap fish or force them into a narrow channel where they can easily be netted.

INDEX

PICTURE CREDITS

American Antiquarian Society, Worcester, Massachusetts, page 29; Jim Baker, Aberdeen, Washington, *Daily World*, page 103; Courtesy of the Thomas Burke Memorial Washington State Museum, (catalog # 2-3844) page 68 (catalog # 1-5257) pages 68–69 (catalog # 2-5E1650) page 69 (top) (catalog # 25.0/145) page 70, (catalog # 1-11183) pages 70–71, (catalog # 1-11184) page 71 (top) (catalog # 1-11181) page 71 (bottom) (catalog # 1-11187) page 72 (top) (catalog # 1-11182) page 72 (bottom); Michael Latil Photography, courtesy Smithsonian Institution, cover, pages 65, 66, 66–67, 67, 69 (bottom); Library of Congress, pages 23, 26, 27, 51, 74, 86, 88, 91; Courtesy of Hazel McKinney, page 102; Museum of the American Indian, Heye Foundation, page 22; Oregon Historical Society, pages 5, 15, 24, 30, 33, 34, 36, 38, 41, 46, 48, 53, 54, 60, 62, 75, 77, 78, 79, 80, 83, 85, 92, 95, 96, 98; Oregon Historical Society, Max Gutierrez, page 99; Oregon Province Archives, Crosby Library, Gonzaga University, page 57; Smithsonian Institution, cover, page 52; Courtesy of Stark Museum of Art, Orange, Texas, pages 16, 21; University of Washington Libraries, Special Collections Division, pages 12, 18, 31, 43, 73.

Maps (pages 2, 39, 101) by Gary Tong.

CLIFFORD E. TRAFZER, a member of the Wyandot Indian tribe, is professor and chair of American Indian Studies at San Diego State University. He is a member of the California Native American Heritage Commission and of the Board of Directors of the San Diego American Indian Health Center. He is the author of several books, including *Renegade Tribe* (with Richard Scheuerman), *The Kit Carson Campaign, Creation of a California Tribe*, and a series of children's books about American Indians.

FRANK W. PORTER III, general editor of INDIANS OF NORTH AMERICA, is director of the Chelsea House Foundation for American Indian Studies. He holds a B.A., M.A., and Ph.D. from the University of Maryland. He has done extensive research concerning the Indians of Maryland and Delaware and is the author of numerous articles on their history, archaeology, geography, and ethnography. He was formerly director of the Maryland Commission on Indian Affairs and American Indian Research and Resource Institute, Gettysburg, Pennsylvania, and he has received grants from the Delaware Humanities Forum, the Maryland Committee for the Humanities, the Ford Foundation, and the National Endowment for the Humanities, among others. Dr. Porter is the author of *The Bureau of Indian Affairs* in the Chelsea House KNOW YOUR GOVERNMENT series.